Reduced
Reflections

Other books by the same author

Fiction

Novels
Conflict in the Home
Sauce of Life
Struggle Toward Extinction
Motivating Forces

Poetry
Diverse Modes
Poems (Flowery Country/Sun and Rain/Grains of Sand)

Non-Fiction

Memoir
Dark Days

Philosophy
Intrinsic to Universe
The Material Structure

Linguistics
LUIF: A New Language
LUIF Dictionaries

Reduced Reflections

TAN KHENG YEANG

Order this book online at www.trafford.com
or email orders@trafford.com

Most Trafford titles are also available at major online book retailers.

Printed in the United States of America.

ISBN: 978-1-4269-5420-7 (sc)
ISBN: 978-1-4269-5421-4 (hc)
ISBN: 978-1-4269-5422-1 (e)

Library of Congress Control Number: 2011900184

Trafford rev. 02/23/2011

 www.trafford.com

North America & International
toll-free: 1 888 232 4444 (USA & Canada)
phone: 250 383 6864 ♦ fax: 812 355 4082

Acknowledgement

"The author wishes to thank Ms. Chao Wei Yang and Ms. Valerie Cameron for their invaluable assistance in preparing the manuscript of this book for publication."

Introduction

This book consists of an assortment of unrelated remarks on a variety of themes. It is not an anthology of sayings culled from various authors; instead, it is intended to be an original composition expressing the writer's view on humankind and the universe. Each remark may be termed a dictum, using this word in the sense of something said, not in the sense of an authoritative saying. A dictum may consist of a phrase, sentence, or paragraph. It may be an observation, maxim, witticism, or felicitous expression.

The writing of dicta differs fundamentally from other forms of composition in that one does not have to concentrate on expatiating at length on a subject but flits from topic to topic, making just a few observations on each. The seemingly casual remarks possess their own peculiar flavour by virtue of their brevity. Among the good points one can think of is the avoidance of padding and garrulity. It is amazing how many authors can spin page after page about nothing, principally because they must bring their books to a respectable length.

A dictum need not necessarily be couched in memorable language, though it is more striking if so done. A good example is the epigram. However, a succession of epigrams would appear artificial and wearisome. Variety, as in everything else, is needed. There is no limitation on what constitutes a dictum. It may be any kind of idea embedded in any mode of expression. Freedom is its essence, and any attempt to control it only serves to throttle it.

Every literary genre serves a specific purpose. What is the aim of writing a book of dicta? It is to record one's thoughts over a wide range of subjects. A dictum is fundamentally a comment—on man and his behaviours, society and its ways, or natural phenomena. Dicta are more memorable than, say, essays. They can be read at any odd moment, and any page can be turned to, there being no continuity of subject matter that would necessitate perusing a book from its commencement and plodding on to its end. They can be found scattered here and there in the works of an author and are often his best-remembered words. A book devoted solely to them makes this type of composition systematic and comprehensive.

A

ABSENCE

Absence is a slow manufacturer of apathy.

One is more concerned with a neighbour one sees daily than with a relative in a distant country.

One should always try not to be absent when one should be present.

The absent make easy scapegoats.

ABSENTMINDEDNESS

We can say one is absentminded when one goes around searching for the shoes that are on one's feet.

Absentmindedness is the penalty imposed on the mind for its crime of concentration on one subject.

People given to fits of absentmindedness have to learn not to be embarrassed by the ridiculous situation in which they are apt to find themselves.

ACCIDENT

Laxity fashions accidents.

A happy accident gives twice as much joy as a happy incident.

He who does not enter a jungle will not accidentally encounter a tiger. Accidents can be courted or avoided.

If a person has a tendency to run into distressing accidents, he blames them on his bad luck. He should sit down and analyse them, and he may then discover that they are due at least partially to his character.

ACCURACY

Practise accuracy at all times, even when it is not absolutely required.

Accuracy gives an impression of truth.

Accuracy is the virtue of mathematics par excellence. It is not so perfect in other connections, but it can be made sufficient for most purposes.

ACQUISITION

The acquisition of money is the raison d'être of most people.

The acquisition of knowledge is what should give the greatest satisfaction.

The acquisition of an evil habit is the prelude to self-destruction.

ACTING

Everyone acts a part in life, for left to nature, he would not be behaving as he does.

Acting is pretence elevated into an art.

ACTION

Action brings thought to the masses.

Action, to be most effective, must be informed by effective thought.

Whatever you do, do it dispiritedly—and you will never live a happy life!

To do one's best is not difficult if the little that one does ordinarily is the best one can do.

It is not always easy to do nothing, for total inaction is alien to human nature.

It is good to review frequently one's actions, scrutinizing the mistakes and faults so as to avoid repetition of them.

A person of action is one given to making firm decisions, whether right or wrong—usually wrong.

ADMIRATION

Numerous are the persons whom the world admires, but few are the truly admirable.

People only admire what they can appreciate.

ADMISSION

One who readily admits guilt does so because he thinks he will not be punished for it.

ADVENTURE

Adventure is more exciting in the recollection than the experience.

Before setting out on an adventure, a sensible person fortifies himself with some courage and much equipment.

Adventure never appears as romantic as to the stay-at-home.

Adventure without an objective is merely bravado.

ADVERSITY

Fallen prosperity embitters a person; adversity that has never known better days is resigned.

Adversity is enjoyable only to the prosperous.

Adversity wears its best aspect in a life of dignity.

Adversity makes it ironic for a person preoccupied with the struggle for daily needs to think of the sublime.

Adversity does not engender crime. It is not adversity but lack of moral fibre that is the cause. Attribution of a crime to adversity does not excuse it.

ADVERTISEMENT

Advertisement transforms bad products into good ones with its magic wand.

Advertisement is the sire of popularity.

Big advertisement speaks small worth.

Advertisements are concerned principally with commodities, but they reflect the prevailing beliefs about life and its purpose.

If there were not so many advertisements, they would be less exasperating.

ADVICE

The best advice is actual aid.

Advice is apt to be freely dispensed because it costs nothing. For the same reason, it is seldom sought and still more rarely taken.

The advice that the giver gives is usually what the recipient already knows.

Advice can be of such a nature that if adopted, it works injury. It needs to be weighed before it is practised.

AFFECTATION

Affectation is always bad, even affectation of what is bad.

Affectation of behaviour, deemed elegant, never fails to excite derisive amusement.

AFFECTION

Affection is never wrong.

Affection generates affection.

The tragedy of affection is when it comes to an end.

Affection is the sunshine of the mind.

Affection is a treasure more difficult to acquire than gold.

AGE

Age must affect the body but need not affect the mind.

Every age is right in its way.

The assumption that when people attain a certain age they should be retired to lead an idle and possibly dependent life because they are presumed to be useless is absurd. They should work as long as they are willing and able to do so.

Old age is an achievement in itself. Every person is young once, but not every person lives to be old.

AGREEMENT

Agreement with others may ensure popularity, but if it is at the expense of intellectual honesty, it is reprehensible.

In business and in politics, people should be as wary of those who agree with them as of those who disagree with them.

The most truculent person does not disagree with his boss.

AIR

About the only thing that all people enjoy in common is the air.

ALARM

A person easily alarmed lives in misery.

ALCOHOL

It's odd that people should destroy themselves with drinking. Alcohol does not drown sorrow but augments it; it does not confer pleasure but engenders misery.

The idea that an ability to stand alcohol is manly is preposterous; what is there manly in swallowing a liquid that makes a person stupid?

Wine in moderation resembles a sportive breeze; in excess, a raging tempest.

Of all the things ingested by humans, alcohol is the silliest.

ALTRUISM

Altruism is service rendered to others without thought of return. This is the highest virtue.

Group loyalty—be it to family, school, association, party, community, or country—is the most popular of virtues because it is the most selfish.

Altruism is the rarest of jewels.

AMATEUR

To do for love what others do for money makes the amateur superior to the professional.

Great work always breathes the spirit of the amateur.

It is customary to speak derogatorily of amateurs, for it is assumed that they possess less knowledge or skill than professionals. But many a professional is merely an amateur who has achieved success.

AMBITION

Ambition for external distinction is far more popular than ambition for internal greatness.

Ambition gives force to character and meaning to practical life. In its absence, life tends to be dull.

Ambition cannot be the bedfellow of modesty.

An ambition achieved loses the enchantment of an ambition entertained.

An ambition that depends on money for its success has to jump over two hurdles: money and success.

AMUSEMENT

The best amusement is one that contains a serious core.

What is an amusement to one person is a bore to another.

Constant amusement soon palls and later appals.

Some amusement to one's taste is the tonic of life.

Perpetual pursuit of amusement is frivolity run riot.

ANCESTRY

It is idle speculating over one's ancestry, and it is meaningless boasting of it. Everybody has to stand on his own feet.

We owe to our descendants what we owe to our ancestors.

ANGER

Anger is not immoral, but it is unpleasant.

Anger gushes from unsure superiority.

An angry person is like a boiling kettle of water.

ANIMAL

The astonishing variety of animal forms shows nature's usual prodigality.

Animal life is a tragedy and nature's mistake. Life should not have been made to feed on life.

ANSWER

One who answers yes when it should be no is submissive; one who answers no when it should be yes is perverse.

Giving a sensible answer to a foolish question is rarer than giving a foolish answer to a sensible question.

ANTIQUE

An antique is a modern treasure.

APPAREL

Apparel is the most apparent thing about a person.

One of the vagaries of fashion is to wear clothing that suggests lack of clothing. It would seem that the purpose of being clothed is to be unclothed.

APPEARANCE

Appearance may correspond with reality and it may not. Knowledge of appearance is instantaneous; knowledge of reality is slow. Taking appearance for reality is a common mistake. If only reality were always as it appears, life would lose its problems.

An ugly appearance spontaneously breeds an adverse reaction; but seekers after truth should conquer their prejudice, for the hideous may conceal the valuable.

APPEASEMENT

Love a tiger and it will still eat you. There are some natures that are incorrigible.

The appeasement of a bully only serves to make him a greater bully.

An aspiring conqueror who has the upper hand is as likely to be softened by appeasement as a raging storm by cowering trees.

APPROPRIATENESS

Action that is appropriate to the time and place will not engender baleful repercussions.

An appropriate remark can save a nasty situation.

An appropriate action may thwart a peril.

Only a fictional character could know the appropriate thing to do under all circumstances.

ARGUMENTATION

Argumentation is the art of presentation and concealment.

Every belief has arguments for and against it.

Argumentation is a futile way of arriving at the truth. No one is ever convinced by it unless he wants to be convinced.

Crooked arguments are far more common than the valid, and they are just as persuasive to the holders of the belief in support of which they are advanced.

Citing an authority or appeal to popularity is not valid argumentation, but they account for the opinions of the generality of mankind.

A vociferous person makes a spectacle of himself and convinces nobody.

ART

Art is an addendum to nature.

Art is the product of the interaction between personality and the external world.

Art is creative only in the sense that it produces fresh patterns of ideas. It does not create something out of nothing or even transform the tangible.

Art is its own purpose. It should not mainly promote extraneous objectives like those of the state or religion.

Although it is not the aim of art to subserve morality, neither should it be its aim to subserve immorality. Degenerate artists are degenerate people, and their art cannot excuse their character.

ASPIRATION

The nature of his aspirations is the criterion of a person's mind.

A lofty aspiration ennobles the lowliest person.

Those who fail in the attainment of their aspirations need not regret overmuch, for these failures have given meaning to their lives.

ATTACK

To attack an unprepared opponent by surprise smacks not of cleverness but of deceitfulness.

In an emergency, the best weapon of attack is the one at hand.

To attack without adequate preparation is folly.

ATTEMPT

Few even attempt to be great.

Effort can never be wasted, for at least it brings experience.

To attempt to accomplish an ideal and fail is better than to accept supinely the actual circumstances.

When undecided, make an attempt.

Effort makes one alive.

Success may elude someone who makes an effort, but it will certainly not come to one who makes none.

ATTENTION

A scandal gets more attention than a good deed.

Nothing wounds a professor's vanity more than lack of attention on the part of his students.

ATTITUDE

A person may have little direction over circumstances, but he can control his reaction. His attitude determines whether the circumstances conquer him or he conquers the circumstances.

One's attitude towards life influences what one will make of it.

ATTRACTION

There is no idea so ludicrous that it fails to attract believers.

The things that attract a person reveal his innermost being.

One should not be ensnared by valueless attractions.

AVERAGE

The average does not give a true idea of heights and depths.

In many things, it is not the average that matters but the heights attainable. The average standard of painting in a country in a particular age is of no interest to anybody; what captivate our minds are the great works of art.

B

BABEL

The world contains a veritable Babel of languages. It is astonishing to see how every community, however savage, could create a language. The multitude of existing languages—with their varying degrees of complexity and difficulty, and all equally unsystematic—divides the human race into labelled division. The label of language produces a Babel of incomprehensible communication.

BABY

A baby is a bundle of untroubling trouble to its mother.

The helplessness of a baby is its strength. None but a hardened scoundrel would injure it.

BACKBITING

Backbiting is the sister of scandal-mongering.

Backbiting is a poisoned dart thrown from ambush.

BADNESS

Nobody is bad in every respect.

What is bad to one person may be good to another.

It is an unfortunate fact that with progress in knowledge, the bad do not vanish. They merely change their modes of operation to suit the new conditions and utilize the latest techniques.

BAFFLING

Much that is baffling can be overcome by determination.

The mind should remain unbaffled by a baffling situation.

BAIT

Fish fall for bait because they can't think; humans fall for bait though they can think.

Bait is danger in disguise.

Bait is brother to deceit.

One should be on guard against an attractive offer without sufficient reason to justify it.

BALANCE

A balance of interests is difficult to maintain. One group will always try to gain more than another.

He who can balance his income and expenditure in inflationary times is hardly less remarkable than he who can balance himself on a tightrope.

BANK

A bank is an unproductive institution for making money from money.

BANQUET

Many people like banquets, especially when they are invited to them.

A banquet is only as good as one can enjoy it.

A banquet is for show; a simple meal of one's favourite food tastes better.

BARBARISM

Barbarism is an ignoble stage of society, and revival of its characteristics is about as sensible as a Barmecide feast.

To stigmatize as barbarism a civilization of which one knew nothing was common in previous ages. It smacked of barbaric ignorance.

BARGAIN

To buy something cheap for its kind is a bargain, but it is not a good bargain if one would normally purchase a more inexpensive article just as serviceable for one's purpose.

BEAUTY

Beauty is nature's signature.

Visible beauty is a matter of appearance, of the harmony of parts, of form, shape, and colour.

Beauty is its own justification; it need have no purpose, no value expressed in other terms.

Beauty perceived by the eye is dazzling; apprehended by the intellect, sublime.

All beauty is transient, whether it pertains to living things or inanimate phenomena.

Human beauty is the normal par excellence. It is the image projected from the physical traits that are characteristic of a people.

BEGGAR

A beggar does not indulge in repartee.

BEGINNING

Many a good beginning stops there.

To end at the beginning of an enterprise is wise if one realizes that one has made a mistake and there is no point proceeding further.

To begin and to end are difficult undertakings.

It is better to have a bad beginning and a good ending than a good beginning and a bad ending.

Everything should be judged by taking into consideration its entire course from beginning to end.

BEHAVIOUR

Behaviour can be character revealed or character concealed.

People behave differently towards different persons.

Few persons deliberately formulate a code of behaviour, and if they did, they could not enumerate all the details. Nobody's behaviour is consistent, except in a novel.

Every person has the behaviour demanded by his character. This does not mean that his behaviour is an accurate reflection of his character, for one of his traits is dissimulation.

To behave well out of character for a short time is easy; to keep it up is difficult.

If you want others to behave well, first do it yourself.

Behaviour cold as a refrigerator is not charismatic.

Unusual behaviour always elicits adverse comment.

In any society, much of the conduct viewed as sensible is senseless.

BELIEF

Irrational belief is most indomitably maintained.

Belief is the precursor of action.

Every person is rich in the inheritance of beliefs.

A passionate belief is one generally born of passion and is quite untrue.

People may not practise what they believe because thought, volition, and action are disparate phenomena.

BENEFIT

No benefit is worth gaining at the expense of the right.

An ostensible benefit may encircle an actual loss.

One crucial benefit, though seemingly small, may mean all the difference between success and failure.

The generous person is eager to confer benefits and reluctant to receive them.

BENEVOLENCE

Were benevolence universal, it would go a long way towards making the world function happily.

Benevolence is far from being a common quality; in practice, it displays only a faint shadow.

A good deed does not necessarily proceed from a benevolent motive.

BIOGRAPHY

Biography is a story arranged to resemble fiction.

No two lives are exactly the same.

An absorbing biography is the work of two persons: the subject and the writer.

BIRD

The bird in a cage lives for people's pleasure, not its own.

A bird is the symbol of freedom.

The eagle, a bird of prey, should not be an object of admiration.

BLACKMAIL

The meanest crime is blackmail.

A blackmailer endeavours to make a fortune out of another's crime. He is an accessory for concealing the fact and a parasite of the most despicable kind. He is worse than his victim.

BLAME

Frustration is the begetter of blame. To be falsely blamed makes one truly angry.

Blaming oneself is in most cases more correct than blaming others.

BODY

A strong body may have a weak mind.

A body is an activated mass of matter.

The voice is the trumpet of the body.

A body is so fragile that it can die from a multitude of causes, from lack of air or food to germs and bullets.

BOOK

A book is a cabinet of thought and experience.

Books are for knowledge and recreation.

It is paradoxical that books, which are the most precious products of humankind, should be cheap compared to other commodities. It is astonishing that in times of scarcity and war, cigarettes and books should greatly increase and decrease in price, respectively. The crux of the problem is that, in spite of progress, people still prefer corporeal enjoyment to intellectual fare.

One book well digested is worth a score rapidly run through.

BORE

The bore is a pathetic creature who fails in his efforts to please.

A bore has the maddening knack of transforming a short story into a novel.

One should not talk like a damaged tap with the water unable to stop running.

A bore thinks that his voice is music; and so it is—the soporific sort.

BOTHER

If people were bothered about what others think of them and could read others' minds, they would be living in a cauldron of bother.

To avoid bother, begin by not bothering others.

Small minds are addicted to bother.

One given to bothering people is as welcome as a fly.

Away with bother and on with action.

Futility and bother are pals, and those who want to eliminate the former should suppress the latter.

BRIBERY

Bribery is unfair payment for a service or payment for an unfair service.

When bribery is rampant and a government cannot eliminate it, the people should eliminate the government.

An official may take bribes a hundred times and escape detection, but once caught, his life is ruined. Corruption is stupidity.

BUILDING

A building is the most durable and the biggest of the material productions of humankind.

A country's achievements are exemplified in its buildings.

A building should be primarily for utility and secondarily for beauty.

Buildings make a town and society.

BULLY

A bully succumbs only to superior force.

The greatest of bullies is one who hides behind a uniform.

The timid is the sire of the bully.

BURDEN

A burden blithely borne is no burden.

No burden is so great as a child to its parents and none so lightly felt.

A politician or official who considers that his job is a burden, but who cannot relinquish it because of a sense of duty to stick to it, deserves to be forcibly relieved of it.

BUREAUCRACY

A bureaucrat is one who gets paid for insolent indolence.

Go to an official for some information and you will find yourself visiting a fair number of the species.

A bureaucracy is the great exponent of waste.

In a public office, work and play are indistinguishable.

BUSINESS

A business that has no business has no business to exist.

The world of business is the world of competition, without which service gravitates towards the slipshod.

Money is the idol of business.

To make a religion of business shows to what bathetic depths humans can sink.

Business for business' sake is an idiocy for it has no value in itself.

C

CALMITY

Nobody is more calamitous than a prophesier of calamities.

Natural calamities are bad, but man-made calamities are worse, if only because human cruelty adds its own dimension of anguish to the mind.

Humankind has never been without calamities.

CALUMNY

Calumny generally leaves a reputation besmirched.

Calumny mixed with truth is the subtlest of poisons.

CAPRICE

Caprice is as vexatious as a guest who drops in at all sorts of uncertain hours.

Caprice is the toy of the nincompoop.

Caprice holds about as much reason as a chameleon.

The capricious will not fail to accumulate a medley of follies.

CARE

Endless care spells endless misery.

When you have a problem, ponder over it, come to a firm decision, be it right or wrong, and keep care at a careful distance.

CATERPILLAR

The ugly caterpillar becomes the beautiful butterfly. Change of a fundamental character is to be expected in human affairs.

CAUSE

When a cause must needs give rise to one and only one effect, the effect is contained in the cause.

The effect need not be commensurate with the cause.

One never does anything without cause, although one may not be aware of it.

After an event has occurred, it is easy to assign a cause; but before it happened, we could not tell whether the supposed cause was sure to give rise to it.

CAUTION

Excessive caution checks enterprise.

Caution is good, but venturesomeness is desirable too.

Reflect before doing anything significant; review after doing anything less significant.

Beware of small mistakes, as they might lead to big tragedies.

CENSURE

Censure is never received with pleasure.

Weigh your censure carefully first, and you may find you have no cause for delivering it.

CEREMONY

Ceremony stifles sense.

Ceremony is designed to inflate the balloon of importance.

CERTAINITY

Seeking absolute certainty in an uncertain world is quixotic.

It is more comforting to be certain than to be uncertain.

Habituation creates the certainty that no reason or unreason is able to shake.

CESSATION

Cessation of a good brings a pang.

CHANCE

When chance confers a benefit on people, they are said to be lucky, as though there were something special in them. In fact, the benefit could have happened to anybody else.

From the standpoint of the individual, his life is determined by chance.

Nature has no place for chance.

CHANGE

Change is good unless it is definitely for the worse.

Change is inherent in the material world. A mountain endures for ages but not without change.

If our ancestors were to come alive today, they would think we are living in a world of magic.

CHAOS

Chaos is the brother of discord.

Chaos never vanishes without leaving behind dire footprints.

CHARACTER

Every person is a miscellany of good and bad, but the proportions are different.

Character makes the person.

Character can be moulded, but the substance is the same.

The character of the individual should not be too characteristic of the group.

Every action has its reaction on character, though we may not be aware of it.

A person's true character can never be known so long as he has to consider legal and social restraints.

CHARITY

Charity is the prop of a bad society.

A person who lives on charity is living on sufferance.

Charity is the most bruited of the virtues because it involves what to most persons is the most precious of articles, to wit, money.

CHEAT

When a cheat gets cheated, he feels sore.

The cheat has a rich collection of promises and a poor recollection of them.

A cheat succeeds by breaking a trust.

Meanness can sink no further than to the level of the cheat.

CHEERFULNESS

The perennially cheerful person refuses to wander away from the shallows of life.

CHILDREN

Children should be guided, not beaten. They should be taught, not oppressed. But they should not be permitted to be pests.

Children should not be treated as though their stage of development were purely a preparation for the future; their activities should be so regulated as partly to fulfil their present needs.

Children live in the present; they do not regret the past or fear the future.

CHOICE

No choice is infallible. When irresolution is prolonged, choose anything.

To make the best use of one's money amid the welter of commodities, one must not only know what one wants but what one prefers.

Nothing is more comic and pathetic than to have to make a show of choice when there is none.

CINEMA

A cinema is a good public place for going to sleep. No one will notice it unless you snore.

Cinema pictures are as sensible or trivial as the public wants them.

CIRCUMSTANCE

Circumstance shapes the behaviour of emperors and beggars.

Circumstance can be quite deceptive; it points to a certain conclusion that yet is erroneous.

CIVILIZATION

Civilization is not a mere matter of refinement; it is the structure of life at its appropriate stage of evolution.

Out of barbarism came civilization, like rain from cloud.

The course of civilization is rugged.

It is absurd to identify civilization with any particular trait or judge of its worth by it.

Civilization abounds with nonsense.

CLEANLINESS

Animals and savages are not given to cleanliness in this world of dirt.

Cleanliness should be the aim for mind and body alike.

CLEVERNESS

Be clever only if necessary or you may find yourself in a mess of trouble.

The truly clever person doesn't want people to know how clever he is.

The clever are inferior to the good.

Cleverness that comes of taking advantage of the morality of others is of a grovelling nature.

CLOTHING

One's clothing is made for the sake of others.

Clothing is the example par excellence of later ornamentation overwhelming earlier utility.

COINCIDENCE

Coincidence may be rare, but it's not impossible.

Coincidence always appears strange and incredible, yet, when one comes to think of it, in the multitudinous details of life, it is odd that coincidences are not more common.

The use of coincidence in fiction to solve problems is not a legitimate device, not because coincidence does not occur in real life, but because it does not so aptly solve problems.

COMMERCIALISM

A thing of beauty fetches a lot of money.

The vulgar hand of commercialism defiles the sublime.

COMMITTEE

A committee is a collection of common people without common sense or of specialists sunk in senselessness.

Nothing moves in such slow motion as a committee.

Where it takes an individual one day to come to a decision, it takes a committee one year to come to no decision.

A committee is the most destructive force in the world; it destroys paper.

COMMON SENSE

Common sense serves for common purposes.

Common sense has been submerged by irrational religions, false ideologies, and ridiculous beliefs.

COMPARISON

Appraisal of worth is a matter of comparison.

A slave who receives daily floggings deems a mere knock on the head an act of kindness.

He who has much needs much to feel happier; he who has little needs little to be happier.

Pain after pleasure is doubly painful.

COMPENSATION

Compensation is poor consolation.

The best compensation for failure is to try again.

COMPETITION

Competition is sweet and sour—sweet for victory and sour for defeat.

One who can take a rival's success without chagrin is more difficult to find than an honest person.

Competition is useful to bring forth the best in a person but it is apt to breed rancour.

COMPLAINT

Complaint is the guitar of disappointment.

Complaint seldom inspires aid.

COMPLETION

To leave a thing hanging in the air is to invite the possible disaster of its falling to the ground and getting shattered.

One project completed is better than ten left unfinished.

One who completes nothing secures no benefit.

COMPLIMENT

The compliment is the child of courtesy and the playmate of respect.

COMPROMISE

Compromise delights nobody but everybody is forced to be satisfied.

Compromise is good in the realm of action but bad in the realm of thought.

COMPULSION

Where compulsion fails and persuasion succeeds, we are astonished and proceed to state that persuasion is more effective, with the implication that this is a general rule. The truth is that usually compulsion can get results more easily than persuasion.

CONCEIT

People dislike conceit in others because they dislike others' success and they fear the conceit might reflect reality.

Conceit need not be offensive; it is so only if it generates injurious behaviour.

All great people are conceited; it is unbelievable that they would go on to the things they do if they did not entertain a high opinion of themselves.

CONCENTRATION

While concentrating on a task, don't disregard the surroundings.

Concentration of thought is to the solution of a problem what honey is to a bee.

CONFIDENCE

Belief in one's ability constitutes half the ability to accomplish a task.

Confidence must have a reasonable basis that needs to be reviewed sometimes.

CONFUSION

Confusion is a creature with an irrational mind in a deformed body.

Confusion creates more confusion.

Confusion is the child of negligence.

CONQUEST

Conquest has been the inglorious lure responsible for half the miseries of mankind.

Conquest is one of those activities where failure is more commendable than success.

CONCSCIENCE

Conscience is a moral code knocked into the brain in childhood.

Conscience is not the incorruptible judge of the mind; it can be bribed by self-interest.

The conscience of few persons is troubled by thoughts of having done wrong. This means that most people are good or their moral standards are set at a low level.

CONSERVATIVE

The conservative of today was the radical of yesterday.

To the conservative, standing still is better sense than moving forward.

The conservative is enamoured of history.

CONSISTENCY

Consistency is harmony, and harmony is beauty. If consistency does not always spell truth, at least it spells beauty. It is a flower with all the parts in unison.

Consistency does not imply truth, but truth implies consistency.

Two mutually contradictory ideas cannot both be right, but they may both be wrong.

CONSOLATION

Consolation can be discovered for everything, if one only cares to search for it. One who has lost his job can find solace in the thought that he is free of meaningless work and can now live in glorious ease.

No consolation is needed if there is no loss.

CONTACT

Contact generates sympathy.

CONTEMPLATION

Contemplation is thought in its purest form.

Contemplation should be active, not passive; its objective is the highest that a person can have—the grasping of the totality of existence.

CONTENT

The joy of content is exaggerated.

Content is for the supine.

Discontent makes for progress; content, for stagnation.

Content is good only where the objective is not worth the struggle.

CONTRAST

Contrast is the microscope of effect.

Contrast is a more emphatic mode of comparison and illustration than similarity.

CONVENTION

It requires considerable unconventionality to be conventional in the traditional way that has become unpopular.

The average person is a creature of convention.

The unconventional person is deemed original; he is rarely so but merely belongs to a minority.

Convention is the sister of fashion.

CONVERSATION

Conversation is the lime of friendship.

Conversation should have some specific purpose. Conversation for conversation's sake is a waste of time.

To speak on trifles the whole day long is bad for the mind and quite common.

Conversation can generate knowledge as well as fatigue.

COOPERATION

The average person is quite cooperative when he cannot help it.

Cooperation works for efficiency and humanity.

CORRUPTION

Corruption destroys society, individual by individual.

Were society not corrupt, there need be no government. But a government is composed of individuals who are corrupt, so corruption is expected to eradicate corruption.

COUNTRY

Division of the world into countries is unnatural.

Birds do not claim any tract of land as their country.

COURAGE

Courage is more prevalent among evil people than among the good.

Cowardice paints pictures more terrifying than the reality would warrant.

Bravery has diverse causes, including resignation to the inevitable, weariness of life, desperation, the effect of wine or drug, vainglory, and superior strength. The best type is when one values life and yet willingly risks it for a good cause.

Danger elicits latent courage, if any.

Little courage, little gain.

Courage and common sense are rarely compatible.

COURTESY

Courtesy is superficial gentleness.

Courtesy is the lubricant of social interaction.

Excessive courtesy, especially of the formalized category, makes one sick.

CRIME

A crime is not necessarily an immorality.

The commencement of the path of crime is a wrong turning.

If crime does not pay, it's because the police are efficient and upright.

The criminal is not criminal in every respect. There is no reason for treating criminals as though everything about them is wrong and they have no rights of any kind.

The criminal is always one step more violent than the law; the harsher the law, the more brutal the criminal.

CRITICISM

To criticise is easy; to achieve is difficult.

Cold criticism is incompatible with ardent appreciation.

People who criticise others for their own good should do the same for themselves.

Criticism gives one a reputation for discernment that is seldom deserved.

One should not baulk at criticism, for it may be critical appreciation.

Criticism is often ignorance tipped with spite.

The best critic is one who understands, appreciates, and says little.

CRUELTY

Cruelty shows humanity at its lowest.

Cruelty is savage and should have vanished with savagedom.

CURIOSITY

Curiosity is the herald of knowledge.

No curiosity, no progress.

Curiosity is linked to interest. One who has no curiosity would find life dull.

CUSTOM

Custom makes the strangest practice seem right.

The tyranny of custom is the most universal of tyrannies and has nothing to justify it. If a custom is wrong, it should be discarded; if it is right, it should be maintained, not because it is a custom, but because the practice is desirable.

CYNICISM

The cynic disdains to entertain illusions about human nature.

Cynicism looks askance at the idols of life.

D

DANGER

Danger gives zest to existence, but most people would prefer not to have it.

It is dangerous to possess what people covet.

He who is addicted to peering down a precipice will topple over it one day.

DAY

Many people think the day is made for rest and the night for action.

A day is long and short, long in sorrow and short in joy.

We should be glad of the days that have elapsed, for if they were sad ones, they are over, and if they were happy ones, we have experienced them.

DEATH

A morbid preoccupation with death poisons life.

Death is the greatest tragedy of humankind.

Death is what shows the insignificance of the individual.

It is preposterous to regard death as other than what it is, a tragedy, but as it is inevitable, it is best to take it stoically.

It would seem futile for humans to pursue any aims, for death ends everything, but things have their sense while they last, and it is not necessary for them to endure forever to be worthwhile.

DEBATE

A debate is a futile exercise for arriving at the truth.

A debate is an argument in formal dress but carried on with the same ignorance, untenable reasoning, and manipulation of facts to score a victory.

DEBT

Businesspeople may borrow to expand their company and emerge winners, but those who enter into debt for personal expense are preparing a pit of ruin for themselves.

Poverty is the sister of debt.

A bill that one is unable to settle is as depressing as a path covered with fallen leaves.

A national debt is worse than a personal debt, for those who borrow are not those who pay.

DECEIT

To deceive a friend is easier than to deceive a stranger, and it is more reprehensible because it involves the betrayal of trust.

Deceit is inglorious to both parties: the deceiver is a rogue, the deceived a simpleton.

Deceit is poison wrapped in chocolate.

The deceiver prefers to crawl through the gloomy tunnels of life rather than to tread with dignity along its sunny highways.

DECISION

Decisiveness wields the sword of firm action.

A firm decision saves torment.

Indecision is the enemy of success.

DEFEAT

Defeat can be more victorious than victory—the touchstone is the soundness of the cause.

Those who continue to struggle are not defeated.

Those who laugh today may cry tomorrow.

The determined person makes defeat a hurdle to surmount.

Those whose eyes are glued to the prospect of easy victory may have their ears assaulted by the din of defeat.

DEFENCE

Defence is seldom wrong, even when it is on behalf of what is wrong.

To move from attack to defence is defeat; to move from defence to attack is victory.

Defence is dictated by necessity; to win, change to attack at the earliest possible moment.

DEFTNESS

Deftness is shown when a speaker abruptly switches to another topic before he reveals his ignorance about what he thought of saying at the time.

Those who are deft with their hands may be skilled craftsmen or skilled thieves.

DEGENERACY

Things do not stand still for long: where progress stops, degeneration ensues.

No society regards itself as degenerate but instead calls itself advanced and enlightened.

Art is no excuse for degeneracy.

DEITY

Deities are the fabrications of ignorance and fear.

Deities are conceived of as benefactors, and the more helpless humans are, the more popular they become. But strangely enough, though the expected help is as often as not missing, belief in them still persists.

DELAY

Delay sometimes solves a problem but more often bungles it.

Delay is seldom planned and despatch seldom unplanned.

DELUSION

A happy delusion has an unhappy ending.

Some people prefer to cherish their delusions rather than to see the truth.

A base person is deluded with a base delusion, a noble person with a noble delusion.

DEMOCRACY

In a democracy, the people suffer for their mistakes; in a dictatorship, they suffer for others' crimes.

Democracy does not imply the existence of parties, which, in fact, are its wreckers.

Democracy does not mean that the views of the majority are right but only that they should be regarded as the norm for the time being.

DEPARTURE

Departure from a happy scene leaves a scar of regret.

To depart in anger is better than to stay and quarrel.

DEPENDENCE

In the last resort, you can depend only on yourself to do what you want.

People are forced to depend on one another whether they recognize it or not.

The individual is dependent on others from birth to death.

One cannot escape some dependence on other persons, but one should cultivate as much independence as possible.

DEPRESSION

A poor person doesn't have to wait for a depression before he has no money to spend.

DESIRE

Desire has no fixed boundaries.

People desire what they can't get and get what they don't desire.

One who permits one's desires to run amok is liable to fall headlong over the precipice of ruin.

A desire unattained continues to be alluring.

DESPAIR

Despair is the poison secreted by the mind when one can't get something one sorely needs.

Despair can supply the energy that hope lacks.

A person doesn't hesitate to climb a tottering tree to escape a tiger; desperation leads to recklessness.

When the outlook appears hopeless, one should still continue the struggle, even if it is only dully, and without being overpowered by despair, for—who knows—things may still change.

DESTRUCTION

The insignificant can destroy the great; termites can bring down an edifice.

DETAIL

If an outline is wrong, the details cannot be right.

Attention to detail is necessary in thought as well as in action, but many details are superfluities.

DETERMINATION

Determination is the rock of success.

The wisest course is to deliberate over a problem from all angles and after arriving at a decision, adhere to it resolutely.

The determined person forges his own tools if necessary.

Determination stifles doubt.

DEVOTION

The fashionable practice is great devotion to money, small devotion to work, and no devotion to duty.

Devotion to an ideal entails the purest happiness.

Devotion to petty pursuits and pleasures is the death knell of a society.

DICTATORSHIP

It is the faulty organization of societies and not any inherent strength in them that allows for the emergence of dictators.

If not for the concept of obedience in the army, police, and civil service, dictatorships would not be so prevalent.

In an absolutist regime, the people are encouraged to air their views after the government has enlightened them regarding the correct ideas.

To autocrats, freedom is an evil, save for themselves.

Dictators believe in discipline, by which they mean obedience to the orders they issue in obedience to themselves.

If a shoemaker became a dictator, he would not make shoes to suit his customers, but he would expect his customers to alter their feet to suit his shoes.

Those who support dictators deserve to be their victims.

DIFFERENCE

People are largely similar, but their differences are exaggerated to have serious consequences.

A harmonious society is one abounding with differences that are not at loggerheads with one another.

To one who is not interested, it makes no difference whether a star is ten or a hundred light years distant.

One little difference can generate immensely different consequences.

DIFFICULTY

Many a grandiose plan is shattered by little difficulties.

What is difficult to achieve is prized, but that doesn't imply that it's valuable.

A difficulty can be eliminated only by grappling with it, not by running away from it.

It is not uncommon to find a task less difficult to execute than envisaged.

DILEMMA

People are in a dilemma when they sport a silly fashion in clothes. Whether it suits them or not, they lose.

It requires great dexterity to overcome a dilemma and one's opponent.

A person faced with a dilemma should think furiously.

DILIGENCE

Diligence never makes one sick.

Trade unions consider that a person willing to work long hours is a disgrace.

Diligence is nature's recommendation for a happy, meaningful life.

DIPLOMACY

Diplomacy is mendacity at the state level.

Diplomacy is the acme of polished and brazen deceit.

A diplomat makes a fine art of the misuse of words.

DISAPPOINTMENT

Repeated disappointments are as erosive as waves on rock.

Harping on one's disappointments does not generate sympathy in others but boredom.

Disappointment would not exercise its trenchant sword so keenly if it were not wholly unexpected.

Those who cannot stand disappointment would do well to avoid dallying with hope.

Life itself is a disappointment.

DISCIPLINE

Discipline is often legalized bullying.

Discipline is the endeavour to compel people to conform to a certain pattern, which may be wrong.

The tyrant in actuality or at heart is most addicted to prating of discipline.

Discipline may be necessary to some extent under certain circumstances, but it is never needed as much as alleged by sadistic disciplinarians and megalomaniac autocrats.

DISCOVERY

Discoveries are not made by those who deem the majority always right.

If a discovery comes to light by chance, it is chance occurring when one is searching for a discovery.

Civilization is the history of discoveries and inventions.

DISCRETION

Discretion is the art of evading troublesome situations.

Discretion is a compound of sense and timidity.

DISSIMULATION

Dissimulation is sister to deceit.

Dissimulation is a lie in action.

Dissimulation is the art of the actor exhibited on the stage of life.

DOUBT

Doubt when there is reason to do so; believe when there is no reason to doubt.

Doubt is a means, not an end.

Doubt comes of ignorance. To dispel doubt, acquire knowledge.

First doubt, then believe.

If all that is dubious were rejected, we would have no beliefs left.

DREAM

Would that to compensate for the miseries of waking life, all dreams were pleasant! A dream can be more terrifying than reality.

There are two faults to avoid: one is to dream dreams and the other is not to do so.

What one dreams of achieving is seldom what one dreams of in sleep, and the former is preferable.

DUTY

Do what you consider your duty and ignore what others say.

One talks loudest of duty who least practises it. Beware of the person who harps on the duty of others.

Duty is often the antithesis of desire and hence its high rate of failure. Where they coincide, it is a hundred percent triumphant.

When people consider that it is their duty to do something that is injurious to others, their duty is suspect.

E

EARNESTNESS

If you are in earnest about your beliefs, they may still not be true, but they are true for you.

An earnest endeavour will go a long way towards solving a problem.

Earnestness and levity have each their proper sphere.

EASE

Not everybody knows how to enjoy ease easily.

In this world, to live at ease forever is not an ideal condition. Human nature being what it is, it would mean ennui and dull misery.

Without sufficient ease, none can be happy.

ECCENTRICITY

Eccentricity is a minor associate of genius.

It is customary to regard eccentric behaviour as abnormal when, in truth, it is conventionalized behaviour that should be deemed strange. Left to themselves, people would develop in their own way; it is due to the force of society that one person unnaturally comes to be so like another.

ECLECTICISM

Truth cannot be found by choosing bits from various systems and inconsistently making a potpourri.

Eclecticism is brother to compromise. It does not work, for in the realm of thought, truth is not a matter of compromise.

ECLIPSE

The eclipse of the sun is more portentous than the eclipse of the moon because it is more conspicuous.

The momentary gloom of an eclipse of the sun is gloomier than night.

The eclipse of prosperity is grievous in that one is haunted by the fear that it may be extinction.

EDUCATION

Education is not confined to schools but accompanies a person everywhere.

Formal education is not necessarily beneficial; it can distort a person for the worse.

Education is the least-appreciated article that parents buy for their children.

An educated person can be as great a fool as a bumpkin but is so in a different way.

EFFICIENCY

Efficiency is maximum output in minimum time.

Efficiency is not a stormy ocean but a gentle river steadily flowing towards the sea.

An efficient mechanic does not have to repair the same fault twice in succession.

EGOTISM

A tumbler of praise from others is worth more than a bucket from oneself.

Egotists are afraid that others may not see them as they see themselves.

EMBARRASSMENT

Embarrassment is an uncomfortable experience, and those who would avoid it have to study their behaviour carefully.

Even the most insensitive of men would be embarrassed if he were chased by his wife around the streets with a boom.

Between friends, it is embarrassing to ask a favour and still more so to refuse to grant it.

EMOTION

Emotion is the heat of the mind.

Emotion supplies action with its kinetic energy.

The essence of art is emotion, which distinguishes it from philosophy and science.

EMPLOYMENT

Many employees who complain that their work is troublesome do not realize that if there were no trouble, they would not be employees.

Hardworking bosses never spare their employees the same treatment.

To the harsh employer, difficulties are excuses.

Long service in one organization may indicate loyalty or the difficulty of finding another job.

ENDURANCE

Endurance rivals the hill in dignity and strength.

The ability to endure pain with patience demonstrates a firm character. Endurance does not denote resignation, and one should continue to struggle towards the objective for which one is temporarily paying the penalty of failure.

ENEMY

Those who would make no enemy must become hermits.

A secret enemy is the most dangerous of enemies; he is a mosquito in the dark.

Strangers seldom become enemies. Those who have no friends have no enemies.

The enmity of even the lowest of people can be dangerous.

ENTERPRISE

The person of enterprise pays no honour to sleep.

Those who would achieve a great enterprise must be prepared to face the numerous difficulties and distresses on the way.

Without enterprise, nothing notable is done.

An enterprising person makes as much money as he can to upkeep the government!

ENVY

Envy is proof of inferiority; the envious person does not possess what another has.

Envy magnifies worth.

The greater the envy, the greater the misery.

The tragedy of envy is its needless misery and its possible introduction to villainy.

Eradicate envy and the world will be a different place.

EQUALITY

In every field of endeavour, there are different degrees of skill between different people.

Two persons are never equal in all respects; neither is one superior to the other in all respects.

There can be no equality where one person has power over another, whatever the equality may be in respect of material possessions.

Artificial equality in respect of rights or property can be enforced by law.

ERROR

One should not slip twice on the same banana peel.

All persons, great or small, make mistakes. One need not be afraid to admit one's errors.

An error uncorrected leads to a string.

An observant individual regards other people's mistakes as vicarious experience from which to learn.

ESCAPE

It is exciting to face danger and pleasurable to escape from it.

To escape from one crisis and confront another is just tough luck.

One should always endeavour to escape from an unjust or intolerable position.

EVIL

Evil is as infectious as cholera.

Evil talk is the herald of evil action.

Goodness is seldom extreme, but villainy is easily so.

Whatever they do, bad people are deemed to do no good; if they show themselves as they are, they are villains; if they act differently from what they are, they are hypocrites.

EVOLUTION

Evolution is progressive change. Seeing that the universe is so imperfect, it would be terrible if it were to remain stationary forever.

Evolution is the practical embodiment of hope.

The triumph of evolution is the triumph of humankind.

EXAGGERATION

Exaggeration is to look at a mouse and proclaim it a squirrel.

Exaggeration falls within the same brackets as mendacity.

EXAMPLE

No example deserves meticulous imitation.

An example to be avoided is as good as one to be imitated.

EXASPERATION

Hardly anything is more exasperating than answering a telephone twice to find it's the same person dialling the wrong number.

To be exasperated is to be miserable, and wise people would immunise themselves from having their peace disturbed by others.

EXCHANGE

Equal exchange is the criterion of justice.

If there were no need of exchange of benefits, there would be no reason for the existence of society.

Taking advantage of others to effect unjust exchange is what causes society to go wrong.

EXCUSE

An excuse can be found for anything.

An excuse derived from the truth is unobjectionable, but many an excuse has unjustifiable justification.

Those who are constantly tendering excuses for their shortcomings would do better to give more thought to their shortcomings and less thought to their excuses.

A right action weighs more in the balance than a dozen excuses.

EXISTENCE

What a person doesn't know doesn't exist for him.

What exists can never cease to exist. It can only change its form.

Existence is the greatest of wonders.

Society does not have a separate existence apart from the individuals who constitute it.

EXPECTATION

To strive for more than one expects will bring less disappointment.

What is usually falls short of what was expected.

Expectation gives transient pleasure, for it ends in sad disappointment or dull fulfilment.

The horizon looks near but it is never reached. Some expectations are unrealizable.

EXPERIENCE

Experience leaves an indelible impression that nothing else can emulate.

Most experience is repetitive and does not extend knowledge. Experience in width counts for more than experience in depth.

Knowledge learned from books or learned from others is the shadow of experience.

When you endeavour to do something, whatever else you may or may not get, you are sure to get at least one thing: experience.

Experience strews the journey of life with its flowers and thorns.

Experience is not sufficient in itself to serve as the lamp of life, for it is restricted in amount and slow in acquisition. It needs to be supplemented by systematic study and earnest reflection.

EXPLANATION

The best explanation is the briefest.

It is not always possible to explain a thing clearly to everybody. A mathematical formula cannot be explained in non-mathematical terms.

An explanation should not be more mysterious than what is to be explained.

EXPLOITATION

The greatest exploiter of the producers is the government.

Exploitation has always existed in one form or another.

No exploitation is more serious than the exploitation of the good.

Exploitation is an unfair transaction.

Judicious exploitation of the earth's natural resources for the good of mankind is the only right exploitation.

EXTRAVAGANCE

Systematic extravagance is popular with rulers and the ruled.

An occasional extravagance gives an inordinate amount of pleasure, which justifies it.

The habitually extravagant travel the downward road to ruin.

The fly of extravagance is liable to get ensnared in the web of insolvency.

F

FACT

Insuppressible facts are the foes of a tyrannical government.

Facts are pins to prick the balloon of error.

Facts are not necessarily clear; if they were, there could be no disputing about them.

Facts are objective phenomena and cannot be distorted, but the difficulty of discerning them allows for wrongful statements of what they are.

FAILURE

Those who try and fail are more commendable than those who never try.

Failure is not synonymous with incompetence.

Failure is a sword that drives the determined person to success.

Failure to execute a nefarious plan incurs less guilt than success.

FAIRNESS

It's easy to be fair when one is not interested.

Fairness in dealing with people never fails to win approbation.

One who has an axe to grind is seldom fair.

Fairness is seldom seen but often heard. No one will admit that he is unfair.

FAITH

Faith is ignorance grown obstinate.

Faith as the criterion of the truth of a creed is about as reliable as a candle flickering in a breeze.

Faith in one's destiny is apt to be rudely shattered.

Faith in the goodness of humankind is pathetic when confronted with its record: malice, swindling, cruelties, rapes, kidnappings, murders, and wars.

FAME

The desire for fame is odd, for a celebrity meets with condemnation as well as praise.

What is striking when said by a celebrity would pass unnoticed if uttered by a nonentity.

FAMILIARITY

The familiar, however absurd, looks right. The unfamiliar, however right, looks mad.

Familiarity blunts the edge of judgment.

FAMILY

The beauty of the family is that it is a permanent refuge from the storms of life.

It is inequitable to extend punishment from a person to his family; it is mean to threaten a person's family for the purpose of compelling him to do what one wants.

FANCY

Fancy creates joy from nothing.

Fancy cannot take the place of reality. Playing the part of a king does not make the actor a king.

Fancy is not objectionable if it does not run riot.

FARMING

Farming is a necessity, not a glory.

FASHION

Fashion is waste of resources for no proper purpose.

Fashion makes temporary idols of the nonsensical.

Fashion is associated with beauty, but its ephemerality shows that the beauty resides only in the imagination.

FATIGUE

Without fatigue, there need be no rest; without work, there would be no fatigue. Fatigue is the intermediary between work and rest.

FAULT

The faultless person is not fit to live in this faulty world.

No good thing is without its faults.

The critic who finds no fault to expose is a nonpareil.

Carelessness is the begetter of faults.

The person who descants on his faults does not think they are serious and, in fact, is secretly proud of them.

FEAR

The spear of fear is the most potent weapon known to humankind.

Fear is the tribute that one pays to power.

Fear is universal; even the tiger slinks away when overcome by dread.

Fear can reduce the strongest person to ignominious behaviour.

Those who say they have no fear of any sort are fibbers.

FEELING

It is too much to expect others to feel for us exactly what we ourselves feel.

There is no reason why one should be ashamed of showing one's feelings.

It is feeling rather than intellect that goes into the making of works of art.

FICTION

The fiction one believes in one calls truth.

The criterion that fiction must not exceed the bounds of possibility or even probability indicates that we are interested only in real life.

Fiction enlarges our conception of the possibilities of existence.

FIGHTING

Fighting is an inglorious exercise.

Nobody has nothing to lose in fighting; one has one's life to lose.

No matter how strong a person is, he can only fight against a very limited number of people.

Bull fights bull and cricket fights cricket. It is more common for people associated in some way to fight one another than for them to fight strangers with whom they have no connection.

FILIAL AFFECTION

The care of parents is the greatest care that one can ever receive. To be unfilial in return contravenes the very essence of justice. To say that one doesn't ask to be born and therefore owes no gratitude is ludicrous; one does not ask to be born a member of a particular country, but betrayal of one's country is stigmatized as treachery.

Children are their parents' greatest joy; should they endeavour to obliterate it?

FIRE

Fire is an ungrateful bully; it consumes its susceptible host.

Fire is beneficial and injurious, good and evil, and is thus quite typical of many phenomena.

FLATTERY

Flattery is the lime to catch a human fly.

Flattery is sweet to the recipient, for to him, it is but praise.

Flattery is at its peak when it appears sincerest.

Flattery consists in pretending that other people are better than they actually are.

The distinction between praise and flattery is the distinction between good and evil. Praise is motivated by sincerity and flattery by deceit.

FLIGHT

Until aviation was discovered, the ability to fly was deemed a magical accomplishment. The aeroplane makes humans surpass the bird in speed of flight. What was impossible became a reality.

Humans can perform the physical feats that other living creatures can, though not as well in respect of each type as some particular species. They can walk, run, leap, climb, and swim. The only thing they cannot do is to fly, but they have made up for this deficiency by their power of invention.

FLY

The persistence of the fly is exasperating. An annoyance becomes unbearable if repeated endlessly.

Do not emulate the stupid bravery of the fly.

FOLLY

The folly of the wise shocks as much as the wisdom of the foolish delights.

Folly is more infectious than wisdom.

Intelligence and folly co-exist in the same person.

When two persons call each other fool, both may be right.

A foolish person is peculiarly foolish if he appears foolish, for most foolish people are not so foolish as to appear foolish.

Even though a person may not mind being a fool, in reality nobody likes to make a fool of himself in public.

FOOD

Humans have to live on food; they don't have to live for food.

Some parties are satiated with too much food, while others are faint with an insufficient amount.

To the starving, leftovers taste like nectar.

No pleasure has so much variety as food.

Although food is a natural necessity, the taste for any particular dish is a cultivated one.

It shows how far humans have advanced from their primeval state when their primary preoccupation with food is overshadowed by their interest in cultural things.

FORCE

Force does not depend on victims for success; other modes of acquiring power require their cooperation.

The weakness of force is that no one has a sufficiency to overcome others permanently. In respect of society, force is artificial. Dictators have none in themselves, but on account of guile and faulty social organization, make use of the force of an organized body to impose themselves on the nation.

Might is distinct from right, and to fail to distinguish between the two is to sink to the nadir of absurdity.

FORTUNE

A person who encounters a misfortune need not be too depressed, for he may obtain something good later on.

Fortune-telling is easy. You just tell people they will enjoy something; if they get it, the prediction is fulfilled, and if they don't get it, the prediction is still fulfilled, for they can enjoy the hope of eventually getting it.

FRANKNESS

A vice does not cease to remain such merely on account of a frank revelation.

Where a vice is fashionable, it is not frankness but vainglory that makes one talk of it.

When people request others to be frank, they expect them to express frankly the sentiments that please them.

Frankness is not necessarily a virtue. To be frank and cause needless distress is surely not right; here, frankness has to yield to the higher virtue of kindness.

FREEDOM

Nothing is an adequate substitute for personal liberty.

One may not be free outwardly but can always be free inwardly.

Individuals enjoy far too little liberty in whatever society they live. Modern governments exercise detailed restrictions in every sphere of activity much more than any despot of past ages. Besides the curbs of the state, society has always interfered with the rights of the individual.

Freedom may mean little to hungry people, but surely they would prefer food with it to food without it. Even if food is more important, it doesn't follow that it can be had only without freedom or that freedom should be banished for good.

A slave is fed, but who would want to be a slave?

FRIENDSHIP

True friendship is a jewel, precious but rare.

A friendship has no tie, natural or artificial; it is as easily broken as it is easily made.

Friendship for company's sake is pleasant; friendship for the sake of assistance is the real thing.

The transition from friendship to hostility can take place in an instant, smoothly, without a pang.

A trifle can sever a friendship of years.

Do not expect your friend to be like yourself.

Too often friendship ends when help is sorely needed!

A stranger can prove more helpful than a friend.

FRIVOLOUSNESS

Frivolousness is odd in a world of hardship and misery.

The frivolous person treats life as a sportive sea wherein he gaily swims, until one day it changes its countenance and lashes him with its turbulent waves.

FURNITURE

A house depends on furniture for its liveability. Things at different levels of importance are complementary.

FUTILITY

Futility is when traffic signs are installed and drivers take scant heed of them.

Whatever is futile is pathetic.

The most futile person is one who dreams dreams and makes no effort to realize them.

FUTURE

The future is the child of the past.

Nothing is more tantalizing than the future.

People have always liked to get acquainted with the future, but unfortunately, the future doesn't like to get acquainted with them.

It might be a good thing that we don't know the future, for if we did, we would have no fresh experience.

G

GAIN

A gain is pleasant but it must be worth the strife.

To forgo a small gain in order to make a bigger is both wise and foolish, depending on one's ability to undertake it.

GAMBLING

Gambling is stationary adventure. The gambler finds as much excitement as the explorer in a strange land but undertakes no physical exertion.

Compulsive gamblers pay for their passion by bankruptcy.

GEM

A gem is a valueless stone made valuable by its rarity.

The beauty of a gem is its only recommendation, but this beauty is not of a lofty or impressive type.

The best gems a person can possess are intellect and character.

GENEROSITY

A person with a reputation for generosity is liable to be beset by supplicants. Anonymous generosity forestalls importunity.

Generosity never hurts, except in the pecuniary way!

Public company directors are generous with the money of the shareholders.

GENIUS

Genius achieves what the ordinary person doesn't consider worth achieving. If genius is admired, it is only when it is accompanied by fame, power or wealth.

Genius is not madness except to the person on the street.

Genius is not a synonym for intelligence or cleverness.

Genius is not an isolated phenomenon. Though it can arise anywhere at any time, it is mainly associated with certain countries in their ages of glory. This shows it is a social product.

Genius is a fortunate misfortune. It brings distress to the individual and progress to society.

GENTLENESS

Those who are gentle to others are gentle to themselves.

Gentleness is as soothing as ferocity is shattering.

Gentleness is as soft as silk.

GETTING

To get something for nothing is a futile dream, by no means uncommon.

If you cannot get what you like, learn to like what you get.

GHOST

Nothing is more horrendous to people than ghosts, and this is odd considering that they are humans in different guise.

The greatest stupidity ever conceived by humans is their creation of ghosts to terrify themselves.

GIFT

To judge a gift by its cost is avarice.

A gift different from what is expected gives no pleasure.

When gifts are too frequent, they cease to excite.

An exchange of gifts is apt to resemble a business transaction.

Gifts seldom persist in the memory.

The greatest gifts a person can have are those with which he is endowed by nature, and these reside in him and persist for life.

GLORY

Genuine glory consists in contribution to human progress.

Inglorious glory is the norm in war and politics.

The glory of ostentation and luxury is but a pale shadow of the genuine article, for it is external and is not intrinsic to a person.

GOLD

More easily will the magnet change its direction than gold its lure!

Honour vanishes where gold intervenes.

GOOD

Good mixed with bad is what normally exists.

When a person desires to do good, we must withhold our judgment and find out what he proposes to do for his brand of good may be evil.

A good person is one who gives you what you want.

GOSSIP

It is irrational to expect gossips to keep a secret, for it is the most interesting part of their chatter.

Scandal is the spiciest item in the bill of fare of gossip and the most popular.

A newspaper yields in efficiency to a gossip.

The essence of gossip is malice.

Credulity is the complement of gossip.

GOVERNMENT

Government is a machine that seldom functions right.

Theory and practice never differ so much as in the matter of government; in theory, the business of government is to govern; in practice, it is to misgovern.

In previous times, governments commonly thought that the way to bring civilization to benighted peoples was to seize their lands; nowadays, governments normally consider that the way to bring happiness to their people is to seize their property.

When a government decides what to do, you have to do what it decides.

The safety of a government is its motive force and accounts for the ferocious cruelty meted out to rebels compared to ordinary criminals.

A government not already rotten from within seldom succumbs to rebels.

GRANDEUR

The grandeur of pomp and power is a ludicrous spectacle of vanity.

The grandeur of a thing is less significant than its worth.

GRATITUDE

Gratitude is, of all human qualities, the least visible. Few are those who pay their debts willingly, and there being no compulsion, the debt of gratitude is seldom paid.

If gratitude were more common, there would be more people to do good. It is all very well to say that one should not expect returns, but it is not human nature to do otherwise and not justice for good to be requited with apathy or evil.

One who constantly reiterates his obligations is merely one kind of flatterer.

GREATNESS

A great person is one who has done something that has chanced to catch the fancy of a people, but that achievement need not necessarily be great, nor is the person who has achieved it great in other respects.

A great person is more of a symbol than an embodiment of value. Whatever that person's achievements may be, his importance in the scheme of things is grossly exaggerated.

GREED

Greed is the uncle of many a failure.

Greed is the whip that lashes people with unhappiness.

Greed and generosity are incompatibles.

GREETING

A greeting is a simple act costing nothing, but it creates goodwill.

A greeting imbued with sincere friendliness is the outward manifestation of benevolence.

A greeting is the first act of social intercourse.

GROWTH

Growth is the cardinal fact of life.

Nothing remains stagnant; whatever stops growing starts declining.

Slow, continual growth is more satisfying than rapid growth, for it lasts longer. Once growth stops, pleasure vanishes.

Institutions grow as though they were living things through the stages from birth to death.

GRUDGE

The injured party does not forget.

A grudge can survive a strangely long time just by feeding on itself.

Victors do not cherish a grudge against their opponents unless they are not convinced of their own superiority.

Help to relatives and friends, instead of evoking gratitude, too often begets grudges because they ask for more than they actually get.

GRUMBLING

Grumbling is the juice from the tree of frustration.

The grumbler blames others for what he can't do.

Chronic grumblers are unhappy people who diffuse misery around themselves.

The tragedy of grumbling resides in its futility.

GUESS

Many a reputation has owed its origin to a lucky guess.

The guess is a potent weapon of thought and action.

A guess is deemed inviolable truth when it becomes the heritage of a people.

GUEST

The time must come when one prefers a guest to depart.

It's terrible to be an unwelcome guest. Apparently there are guests who don't find it terrible because they think the epithet cannot apply to them.

Courtesy is never more necessary than towards a guest.

GUIDE

An ignorant or a villainous guide is worse than no guide.

The best guide is one who shows the way and does not seek to enforce his decision.

One who would guide others along the path of knowledge must possess patience and understanding.

GUILT

Through guilt is hard to prove, the guilty is still guilty.

It is not true to say that the guilty person is apt to display signs of guilt, like running away from the scene of the crime, and that the innocent has nothing to fear. In a world where truth need not ultimately prevail and justice does not necessarily triumph, the innocent have more to fear than the guilty, for if they suffer punishment, they would be suffering for nothing.

H

HABIT

Habit is the brother of inertia.

Habit makes life easy by generating automatic action.

Habit can be changed only by incessant guerrilla warfare.

HALF

If half of all your wishes were fulfilled, you could consider yourself lucky.

Half a fish cannot live.

A task left half done is not done.

HAPPINESS

Happiness issues from the mint of the mind. Each person may find happiness in his own way, according to the nature of his mint.

There are two joys every person should have—the joy of work and the joy of rest.

The happy person is one who does not think of his happiness.

Don't make yourself happy by making others miserable.

HARBOUR

A harbour is to a ship what a nest is to a bird.

A fine harbour sprinkled with crafts of diverse kinds is a poetic scene composed by humankind and nature.

HARDSHIP

Hardship forges a person's character as heat forges iron.

One who has never known hardship has not lived.

Hardship is of the essence of the process of evolution.

Humans inflict hardship upon humans. Some hardships are natural but more are artificial.

Extreme, unremitting hardship leads to death.

HARM

Inadvertent harm brings regret, deliberate harm delight; but to the victim, they are both equally grievous.

Anyone can suffer harm from nature, beast or human.

People should endeavour to avoid harming others and themselves.

HARMONY

Harmony is beauty.

If you would be happy, cultivate harmony.

Harmony is one thing that cannot be achieved by force.

One side alone cannot make harmony.

HARSHNESS

Harshness is sometimes necessary to bring a person to order.

Harshness is a quality as unlovable as pins and needles in the feet.

HASTE

Haste is necessary in an emergency. More haste, better result.

Haste with circumspection is the best procedure in many situations in life.

HATE

Hate is a more effective spur to action than love.

The hatred of evil is only one step less commendable than the love of good.

Hate is to be judged by what it hates.

HEALTH

Health is important but not so important as to merit preoccupation with it.

When one is sick, life wears the robe of misery.

Mankind has never been healthier, and that achievement alone would vindicate science.

The hypochondriac is a nuisance and the malingerer a waster. Both are social menaces.

Some persons are expert in keeping themselves healthy and others equally skilful in making themselves sick.

HELP

The more the cost to the giver, not in terms of money but in terms of sacrifice, the more the debt of help.

Helpful men are common; they either help you or help themselves to what you have.

One should learn to need as little help as possible.

When you help others, do not put on airs of superiority, which only serve to induce embarrassment and resentment.

HEREDITY

An eagle begets an eagle, but a great person may beget a dolt.

HERITAGE

Every society should add to its heritage. It is a sorry age that merely transmits.

HERO

A hero turned villain is the saddest of spectacles.

Heroes by choice become pathetic laughingstocks if they do not know when to retire from their calling.

Hero-worship is the poor relative of autocracy. It must be accounted a fact that the ordinary person tends to admire dictators or they could not establish themselves so easily.

HINT

When a hint is necessary, the affair is unpleasant.

One does not give hints to dogs and dolts.

A direct reference is preferable to a hint.

No person is more exasperating than one who will not take a hint.

HISTORY

History is a romantic tale of crime and folly.

History can never be a record of unvarnished truth, if only for the simple reason that we can never be certain of the motives and incidents behind overt actions.

History is a summary of human achievements and events, but the account is riddled with errors.

Two events in history don't possess a necessary nexus.

History can teach no infallible lessons.

History will repeat itself as long as human nature does the same.

HOBBY

A hobby suggests play. Whatever one does seriously should be regarded as work.

A hobby is justified by the pleasure it gives, even though it appears puerile.

The best hobby combines pleasure and intellectual cultivation or service to society.

HOLIDAY

A regular holiday at frequent intervals becomes an ordinary day.

A holiday from home is delightful, but a holiday at home is more delightful in that it contains the essence of a holiday: rest.

HOME

Home is sweet only when its members live in harmony.

Spending more time at home is having less vexation outside.

In no other place can one be really free and easy save at home, and this constitutes the essence of happiness.

Many people regard home as the place where they go when all other places are closed.

Nostalgia is the only ailment that is commendable.

HONESTY

Honesty as the best policy is not so admirable as honesty as an ethical objective; but whatever the motivation, it is better than dishonesty.

Progress has been made in many ways but not in respect of honesty. If Diogenes were to come alive today, he could trudge through all the cities of the world with his lantern and get no better result than he did twenty-three centuries ago in Athens.

HONEY

He who is intent on gathering the honey of life is more likely to be pricked by its thorns.

HONOUR

That kind of honour that is false pride in little things is better discarded.

True honour does not consist in following a code of honour but in practising humanity and kindness.

Persons who are honourable officially and socially are often dishonourable in actuality.

HOPE

Hope is often a gay deceiver but is sometimes a skilful soothsayer.

Hope glows bright even when conditions are dark.

The wise and the foolish are equally inundated by hope.

Fruition confers no greater joy than hope.

Hope is the first step towards success.

Associate action with hope and hope will then shine more fervently and success will ensue more readily.

HORIZON

That the sky should meet the earth is a strange illusion.

The horizon seems not so far away but is never reached. A desirable something seems easily attainable but somehow forever eludes one's grasp.

HOTEL

Money talks loudest in hotels. The welcome and service generated outweigh what a relative or friend would give.

HOUSE

A house is a utility that can be a work of art.

The ownership of a house secretes a rich latex of satisfaction.

HUMAN BEINGS

Human beings have a variety absent from other animals. Individual differs from individual.

Human beings are animals physically and unique beings mentally.

Human beings cut such a sorry figure with their behaviour that, at first sight, they deserve severe condemnation; but on second thought, they are better treated with sympathy and understanding, for they cannot help their ways.

Human beings are unique in many respects, especially in their having to learn about everything from food to sex, which other animals know instinctively.

Human beings are the measure of all things only for their own purposes.

It is a convenient and flattering fiction for human beings to look at the universe as though it were designed for their behoof.

HUMAN NATURE

Human nature is neither good nor bad but is as made by nature. It is a mixed assortment of qualities, some good, some bad, as judged by any particular moral code.

Human nature may not change, but it can manifest itself in different forms.

HUMANITY

The division of humanity into groups, natural or artificial, has fomented strife and misery. It should not have done so, as the unity of mankind is far more important than the variety of its manifestations.

HUMOUR

Humour is the beverage of the mind.

Humour reduces pretentiousness to its proper level.

Humour illuminates the dark chamber of life.

Where humour is, social intercourse is borne lightly along its current.

HUNGER

Hunger sets people to work.

A sage's words or a peasant's food—which would the hungry prefer?

HUNTING

Hunting is called a sport. No other evidence is needed to show that humans are born fundamentally wrong.

The better the hunter, the worse for the prey.

HURRY

It is queer that the people most in a hurry are those behind the steering wheel of a car when normally they are already proceeding faster than people at other tasks. Apparently, speed begets a hankering for greater speed.

Those who seem to be perpetually in a hurry may have no destination of any moment.

HYPOCRISY

Hypocrites are secret libertines living in a society that roundly condemns their way of life.

No character is funnier than the hypocrite, who lives two lives at odds with each other.

Hypocrisy is pusillanimity motivated by social standing.

I

ICE

Ice is hard, yet it is only solidified water. The protean change of natural phenomena is truly amazing.

Ice does not melt without heat; a problem is not solved without thought.

To meet people with ice in their hands and on their faces is to feel doubly chilled.

IDEA

Ideas are humankind's greatest possession.

Ideas are of no interest to the ordinary person if they cannot breed money.

A popular idea is more powerful than a bomb; an unpopular one, feebler than a feather. Popularity has no connection with truth or grandeur but is a matter of chance and circumstance.

An idea doesn't function of itself.

Heterogeneous ideas are often found associated.

IDEAL

Ideals elevate the mind.

Lack of ideals makes society stationary or retrograde.

An ideal society may be impossible to realise, but it is good to have one in mind.

Those who disdain ideals are fools or villains. They may consider themselves hardheaded realists, but in actuality, their minds are cast in a pedestrian mould.

IDEALOGY

No age can beat the present for love of ideology.

A brutal ideology makes a brutal society.

Savages need no ideology to justify their behaviour. The ostensibly civilized whose behaviour is no different conceal their atavistic instincts behind flimsy ideologies.

An ideology can be overcome only by another ideology and not, at least permanently, by force.

IDLENESS

Complete idleness is impossible to achieve.

Idleness survives at the expense of diligence.

Idleness is not one long holiday, for it is not a pleasure.

IGNORANCE

To the average person, ignorance is more welcome than knowledge for its own sake.

When an ignorant electorate supports an ignorant leadership, what result can be expected save disaster?

The ignorant are not more easily led than the educated. It is more difficult to convince a bumpkin of an idea when he cannot follow the arguments than a scholar who understands what one is talking about.

Ignorance is the most efficient preventive for keeping people from doing what is considered undesirable.

Ignorance is a mirror that reflects nothing.

ILLUSION

People go through life under the sway of illusion.

The net of illusion is delicate but tough.

Those who think they have no illusions have one more illusion.

Illusion is romanticism posing as realism.

IMAGINATION

Imagination is the most active principle of the mind.

It is imagination, not reason, that creates. Imagination has created worlds.

We do not trust imagination to reveal to us the truth, but it has its own uses and should not be disparaged.

Imagination is to life what the rainbow is to the sky.

IMITATION

Imitation is the boon and bane of humans. They are naturally imitative, and this makes for ready leaning as well as a tendency to decry originality.

An imitation, however good, is still an inferior product.

Better than imitation is adaptation.

Rather than imitate other people, it is better to learn to avoid their faults.

IMMUTABILITY

Life would be a disaster if it were immutable.

No phenomenon is immutable, not even the stars. It is a mere hyperbole when a person says his will is immutable.

IMPORTANCE

People are important only when they occupy their familiar, normal position. A monarch who appears in a village incognito would be treated by the peasants like any other stranger.

The person in the street tends to regard as important what is trivial and as trivial what is important.

Quality is a better measure of importance than quantity.

IMPROVEMENT

One should continually strive to improve oneself in every way.

Improvement of his financial position is the only improvement that the average person is eager to seek.

Improvement is never a mistake.

IMPULSE

Impulse is a bad substitute for thought.

To act on impulse is seldom right, but in matters of urgency, it is better to do so than to hesitate.

INDIFFERENCE

Indifference where care is needed is evil; where hostility is expected, it is commendable.

Leaving people to their own resources may be the best way to help them.

The misfortune of indifference is loss. When one does not care for what is of value, like knowledge or culture, one is voluntarily inflicting on oneself a deprivation.

INDIVIDUAL

A crowd is composed of individuals. The individual is a concrete being; the crowd is an abstraction.

To stand with the multitude is easy; to stand with the minority is difficult; to stand alone is phenomenal.

Individuality is a mark of distinction, the jewel of character.

INDUSTRY

Industry being productive should be the foundation of an economy; trade is a minor concern.

The Industrial Revolution has been the greatest single factor in promoting material welfare. It has changed the face of the world.

Industry, mechanical production, is labour at its most sensible.

INFALLIBILITY

Infallibility is an impossibility.

INFLATION

Price is the toy of inflation.

Inflation is so powerful that even the miser realizes that other things may be more valuable than money.

Buy whatever you want and whatever you don't want, for they will cost more soon!

Nothing cuts more keenly than a razor save inflation.

Nothing can look so small as money when prices are rising rapidly.

Inflation deflates the balloon of prosperity.

INFLUENCE

It is easy to be influenced by the company one keeps. Walking along a muddy lane makes the trousers spotted with mud.

One cannot escape the influence of the weather.

Each person is a bundle of influences exerted on him by others in the course of his life.

INFORMATION

A problem is solved if one knows where to get the information.

Verbal information is seldom accurate.

Psychological warfare consists of dishonest information honestly presented.

INSOMNIA

Some compensation may be wrung out of insomnia by utilizing it for thought.

Sleep is time wasted in an unconscious state, and insomnia should properly be welcome—if only it entails no ill effects!

INSPIRATION

Lack of inspiration is the sluggard's excuse. Enthusiasm breeds its inspiration.

One's inspiration lies within oneself.

An inspiring factor merely inspires a person to work; the output can be bad.

What inspires one person doesn't inspire another.

An ideal is the best inspiration.

Spasmodic inspiration is not for practical life, which needs regular work.

Many a man attributes his inspiration to his wife. This is likely to take the form of scepticism!

INSTINCT

Instinct is the king and reason the subject. It should be the other way about.

The instinct to live is the fundamental instinct.

Instincts are natural, but they are not all good. Bad instincts should be eliminated with mental evolution; this is in accordance with the natural trend of the universe.

INSULT

An insult is a wound inflicted on the mind by the spear of contempt.

A mocking insult breeds a revengeful fury out of all proportion to the damage done.

People are most sensitive to verbal insults when they are least liable to physical injury.

Those who easily feel insulted over a lot of things should keep themselves away from society.

A gratuitous insult bespeaks a mean mind.

Insults can be levelled at anybody and anything.

INSURANCE

With accident insurance, one can afford to have accidents!

Insurance does not insure anything with greater certainty than the payment of premiums.

Those who take out a life insurance policy lose on the transaction unless they have the luck to die early!

INTENTION

The result of an action often differs from the intention.

The intention behind an action determines its moral value.

It is easy to entertain a good intention and hard to effect it.

Put an intention into practice without delay.

INTEREST

Interest in another's affairs is not welcome unless it be to praise or help.

Interest in life keeps one alive.

A diversity of interests is the subjugator of tedium.

INTERMEDIARY

The intermediary ends with dislike from one or both parties.

Of all the kind things that one can do, the most thankless task is to act as an intermediary.

INTRIGUE

Intrigue gives society its basest character.

Intrigue is secretive and treacherous and has nothing to commend it.

The less the intrigue, the healthier the state.

INTUITION

When people stress intuition, it is because they want to hold on to a belief for which they can adduce no reason.

Intuition as a tool of knowledge is as unreliable as imagination.

Using intuition as a vindication, one can put forward any theory.

One who relies on intuition to get the truth first gets the truth and then supports it by his intuition.

INVENTION

Invention is creative thought applied to matter.

Inventions benefit all humankind; though some are pernicious, they need not be so.

The accidental invention is the happiest of accidents.

An ingenious invention is not necessarily the most useful; utility determines worth.

Material civilization is the fruit of invention.

An inventor, like any other originator, must be prepared for ridicule.

INVITATION

An insincere invitation is best rejected.

An invitation to secret destruction is the meanest of actions.

An invitation to the poor to attend a party is charity; to the rich it is flattery; to equals it is friendship.

He who receives the most invitations is the one who needs them least.

INVOLVEMENT

It is easy to get involved with a gang of bad hats but difficult to leave them.

Needless involvement in other people's affairs is not a sign of public spirit but of meddlesome curiosity.

IRONY

Irony is meaning taking a somersault.

Irony is humour linked to insult.

It is ironical to hear a person not given to irony give vent to an ironical remark.

J

JARGON

Fondness for jargon is folly masquerading as learning.

Some jargon may be necessary for adequate expression; needless jargon is a pest.

JEALOUSY

Jealousy is possessiveness smarting from a sense of insult.

Jealousy is a sign of inferiority.

Jealousy is kin to malice.

Jealousy is a resourceful inventor of stratagems.

If jealousy is not curbed, it will suffocate the sufferer.

Jealousy in matters of love is a fault and in respect of attainments, an evil.

As much as possible, avoid making people jealous of you in respect of anything, for no enmity is stronger than that motivated by jealousy.

JEST

A jest that contains a truthful sting is a needless cruelty to be avoided.

To speak in jest on serious matters is to lose potential converts.

JOURNALISM

The best use of a newspaper is a wrapper.

Few persons care to read books, but everybody reads newspapers. This proves that reading is not itself a painful task.

The influence of newspapers is great, because most people's minds are receptive vacuums.

Journalists falsify their task when they present not facts but tendentious distortions.

JOURNEY

A short journey is joyous, a long one tiresome.

A journey is most enjoyable at the beginning and the end when expectation and relief respectively dominate.

A journey in company is pleasant, but a journey alone makes one more attentive to the company of nature.

JUDGMENT

The aim of judgment is to get at the truth, and this should transcend technicalities and eloquence.

Nobody is perfect; in assessing people, weigh all their points as a whole.

Those whose interests are not affected will judge impartially.

When those you have been accustomed to dislike suddenly do something beneficial to you, you immediately change your feelings and consider them to be good fellows.

A wrong judgment may yield a right; human fallibility has its good points.

JUGGLERY

Jugglery is a diversion of no value.

Jugglery is an exhibition of skill made before an audience with its critical faculties temporarily suspended by a person, who has spent years mastering a few tricks, which are as devoid of sense as skyrocketing inflation.

JUNGLE

A jungle is a place where life, both vegetable and animal, grows in reckless abandon.

The jungle is the arena of the struggle for existence par excellence.

The law of the jungle is the law of the town, where it is applied in subtler ways.

JUSTICE

Justice whets morale.

The best justice is not stern but sympathetic.

Unjust justice is far from being uncommon in many a law court in the world.

To condone injustice is to condemn justice.

A society without justice is one without sense.

K

KETTLE

The kettle is the intermediary between water and fire; the water doesn't quench the fire but receives its gift of heat. It is a marvellous invention, but like so many others, the inventor is unknown.

KILLING

No killing, private or public, whatever the circumstances may be and under whatever name it is called, is laudable; at best, it is only excusable.

KINDNESS

Kindness is the sugar of society.

Kindness is the most practically beneficial of virtues, and if all people practised it, society would be completely different.

An act of kindness, however small, is not too small to perform.

A kind stranger is better than an unsympathetic relative.

KING

When kings were the order of the day, their frightening power was accepted as natural.

That throughout most of history monarchism flourished and that in modern times dictatorship is popular is evidence of the propensity of humankind to hold power in esteem.

KNAVE

A knave is a wretch who thinks he is clever.

The cleverest knave is liable to trip himself.

The knave is distrusted even by knaves.

KNOT

No knot is so intricate that it cannot be unknotted. No problem can be set so complicated that it cannot be solved.

KNOWLEDGE

Knowledge elevates the possessor.

Knowledge of whatever kind is never wrong.

The aim of knowledge is knowledge. Knowledge is its own raison d'être.

Knowledge of the universe is the highest knowledge of the scheme of things.

Individuals cannot know everything, but they can acquire an outline knowledge of the scheme of things.

The greatest gift of our ancestors is the transmission of their accumulated knowledge. Whatever progress we may make, the sum of our new knowledge is but small compared to our inheritance, from which furthermore ours proceeds.

L

LABEL

People love labels. Individuals are judged by their labels—for example, their sex, age, occupation, or race. We do not think of a person as a complex of qualities but as a collection of labels.

LABOUR

Labour for labour's sake is meaningless. Labour for welfare is labour's justification, inspiration and objective.

Labour should not be regarded as a commodity, though it has a value in exchange because it is the producer of commodities and is part of humankind itself.

LAKE

The most beautiful of waters is a lake.

A lake is an island in reverse.

LAND

Land is the property of nature, and humankind is only the user.

Land is priceless for people, for on it they dwell and from it they draw their sustenance.

If the land could feel, it would marvel at the innumerable creatures that have passed over it in the eons since life came into being.

LANDSCAPE

A landscape is a natural picture.

A landscape is the most beautiful work of nature.

A landscape is most enamouring at sunset.

LANGUAGE

Language is the currency of thought.

Language is not an end in itself.

Of all human contrivances, language has the greatest importance, and it enters into our very being; but it is desirable to reduce and not exaggerate its weightiness, for it is only a vehicle, and we must not mistake it for its passenger.

LATENESS

That which comes late seldom makes exultant.

One who is late is left behind.

LAUGHTER

The laughter of despair is the saddest of human sounds.

Laughter is not necessarily the product of innocent happiness. It could be caused by a variety of factors, like contempt and hatred. Evil laughter is the most nauseating of all sounds.

LAW

Law has been made into the preserver of iniquity.

The frustrating delays of the law are merely a matter of custom and inefficiency.

The laws of present-day states are more multitudinous than pins, and yet every person is presumed to know the laws of the land in which he lives.

People obey the laws because it is their duty and they don't like to go to prison.

The only place where people can be recklessly insulted is a courtroom as, after swearing they will tell the truth, their every statement is doubted by some lawyer.

LEADER

Many a leader is a follower in disguise.

The most pronounced absurdity of leaders is that they have an inclination to act as though they were infallible.

LEARNING

A pedant learns more and more to know less and less.

One should come in contact with different sorts of persons and things, even the bad, not to learn what to do but to learn what not to do.

People can learn from their parents or their children. No person is too old or too young to have no appropriate knowledge to impart.

One may like to learn about something without learning to like it.

LEGEND

A legend was a true story to its early believers.

The imagination has always been a vigorously developed faculty. The proof of this can be seen from the corpus of detailed legends of a people.

To be a living legend is to be constantly on guard that the pose is not brutally shattered by reality.

LEISURE

Leisure determines character more than work.

Leisure is for activity, not rest.

Those who don't know how to spend their leisure should have none.

LETTER

A letter is a slice of autobiography.

A friendly letter is rarely too long and an official letter rarely too short.

A letter from a distant country is travel by proxy.

LIBRARY

An hour in a library is more rewarding than an hour anywhere else.

A public library is the noblest of public benefits.

A library is a record of the adventures of the human mind.

When we enter a library, we enter a world of peace. Whatever the personalities of the authors may be, here they are quiet and they speak to us only if we want to hear them. They can be our friends; they cannot quarrel with us.

LICENCE

Licence is liberty trespassing on another person's right.

Licence is the image of liberty made foul.

Licence is liberty bloated with the desire for power and is more characteristic of the tyrant than the mob.

To a dictator, freedom is licence; to a democrat, any curb on an existent freedom is slavery.

LIFE

The aim of life is to live.

Our view of life is conditioned by our circumstances. If we are happy, we think that life is good; if unhappy, bad.

One of these days, we'll think that life is hard if we couldn't spend an occasional holiday on another planet.

To spend day after day uselessly is a crime against life.

Far too many people take life lightly and death seriously; it would be better to take life seriously and death lightly.

Life is short, but a life without meaning or filled with endless pain is long.

If people were to think and act aright, they could make life one stretch of happiness from childhood to old age.

LIGHT

Light can always dispel darkness.

The fate of life hangs on light.

The light of wisdom is the sublimest light.

LIGHTNING

Danger surrounds us on every slide; even the atmosphere contains a killer. Lightning wields its electrical sword indiscriminately on good and bad alike.

Sudden and fleeting though lightning is, it leaves a striking impression.

LIKING

You like what I like and I like what you like; it's capital, but it's odd.

To do whatever one likes bespeaks lack of will power; to like whatever one does bespeaks lack of judgment.

To do what you like is pleasant; to like what you do is still more pleasant.

LION

The lion is not the biggest or the strongest of animals; its ferocity adds to its power. In the wilds as in human society, violence and not gentleness wins power.

The bravery of the lion is for predacious purposes and does not merit admiration.

LITERATURE

Literature is life in print. It is not a mass of words for professorial dissection.

The literature of a country dies when it is dominated by learned men.

LITTLE

A little might be too much.

A little can wipe out a lot. An error can bring a whole scheme to naught, and a good deed can extinguish all previous enmities.

LIVELIHOOD

Looking around and seeing the number of vocations in the world, some exceedingly strange, one may well ask, "What will a person not do for a living?"

When a person's livelihood is at stake, his behaviour may change from gentle to fierce.

LOAN

The borrower exists without dignity.

Do not lend what you are not prepared to lose.

When a friend gets a loan from you, you begin to wonder after some time whether he intends to return it or retain it.

One who can afford to pay back, even though it be later, seldom has any cause to borrow.

LOSS

To lose what one does not care for is not loss.

It is a profitable loss when from a loss a gain ensues that more than covers it.

Among the generous, the loser excites sympathy; among the vulgar, contempt.

LOTTERY

The purpose of a lottery is to collect from the many and endow the lucky few. This borders dangerously on the concept of an aristocracy.

A lottery is supposed to operate in accordance with pure chance. Some lotteries, however, behave as though chance is a stranger to them.

LOVE

Love, as popularly understood, refers only to sexual love and is employed to camouflage libido. From the use of the word mainly to denote an emotion, which is associated with sexual desire, it is not surprising that psychologists should have come up with the notion that all forms of strong attachment are connected with the generative organs.

Though as an ingredient of human nature, love is basically the same in all climes and ages, it has diverse fashions and ways of expression.

Love, under all circumstances and in perpetuity, is what gives human relationship its greatest strength.

Love that is primarily play is not love but play.

LUCIDITY

The lucidity of a lake is essential to its beauty; lucidity of thought is necessary for its comprehension.

In prose, lucidity is the backbone of style.

LUCK

The expert has all the luck.

When people achieve success, they attribute it to their intelligence; when they meet with failure, to their bad luck.

It is exasperating to find luck going to one's enemies.

If one believes in luck, one need not struggle for success, as it will just come—or so one hopes.

LUXURY

The luxury of yesterday is the necessity of today. It was condemned when it was confined to the few but is deemed innocuous when it is widespread.

A luxury one can easily afford becomes a necessity; a necessity one can ill afford becomes a luxury.

Luxury generates a snobbish glow of satisfaction.

Luxury is as attractive and oppressive as a heavy scent.

LYING

A disadvantage of lying is that one may tell different stories at different times.

A lie and a wrong statement are equally misleading, but they differ in the intention.

A lie that is a complete fabrication without any admixture of fact is uncommon.

Lying for personal gain is evil; lying to avoid causing hurt is excusable; lying as a sport is in bad taste.

Even the worst liar occasionally tells the truth.

M

MACHINE

It is odd that an assemblage of pieces of metal should function more accurately than a living, thinking being. People are natural machines that make artificial machines that outstrip themselves in productivity.

MADNESS

Abnormality is not madness.

It's easy to accuse an individual of madness, but a nation is not so censured for its strange ways.

Insane sanity is more common than sane insanity.

MAGIC

Magic is crude science.

Magic preys on ignorance but gains little.

MALICE

The fact that one is apt to laugh at the misfortunes of others betrays the large extent of malice in human nature.

Malice is a poison to possessor and recipient alike.

The pleasure of malice is more than counterbalanced by its pain.

People tend to put a bad interpretation on one's actions.

MANNERS

Manners are conventions regulating social intercourse. If highly artificial, they are laughable. The best are the spontaneous expressions of kindliness.

Manners are the clothes of character.

MAP

With a map, a stranger can move about any city, however complicated its pattern of streets. The map is the traveller's friend in reticulate garb.

MARKET

The market typifies the daily life of the people.

The market is an innocuous but not an admirable institution. Its hubbub and coarseness show life at its lowest.

MARRIAGE

Marriage is a practical measure in romantic apparel.

A happy wedding is often the prelude to a happier divorce.

For revelation of character, nothing can equal marriage.

Experience does not always make for better performance. A person who has had experience of one marriage is as likely to fail with a second.

A trial marriage is as useful as a weather forecast.

A man and wife of differing temperaments resemble reinforced concrete; he copes with one kind of problem and she with the opposite.

MASS INDOCTRINATION

Mass indoctrination renders all individuals one individual. What one likes, all like.

MATTER

We do not see matter as it is but only its photographs in the mind.

Matter is the greatest of illusionists, for what we see of it is greatly different from what it actually is.

Matter makes life seem more real.

MAXIM

No maxim applies in every case.

One does not mould one's life on maxims, and if one did, one would be not a paragon but a curiosity.

A maxim is a guide, not a dictator.

A maxim is instruction wrapped in a pellet and thrown at the mind.

A maxim demonstrates its worth only when in action.

Maxims are not natural truths. They are made by humans, for the most part in accordance with the prevailing ideas of the age, and may be right or wrong.

MEANING

Obscurity of meaning does not indicate profundity but ignorance. It shows that writers do not know how to express themselves or don't understand the subject.

To mean what one does not mean—to be misunderstood—can give no pleasure.

Meaningless meaning is beloved of those who have nothing to say while penning lengthy passages of convoluted prose.

MEANS

The means should suit the end. It is ridiculous to wrap vegetables in silk or bail water with paper.

To pursue a laudable objective with the right means is the proper policy.

Reason is the only reliable means for the solution of problems.

The sharpest knife can be blunted. The best means can go foul.

MEDICINE

Every ailment has its medicine, if it can be found.

Proper food makes the best medicine.

MEETING

A meeting is a gathering of reluctant persons to pass an unpleasant hour.

One who speaks most at a meeting is as often as not the most deficient in sense.

MEMORY

Memory is the biographer of one's life.

Memory is a romantic poet making ballads of commonplace incidents.

A good memory preserves what the eye observes.

A memory that never forgets is not an undiluted blessing, for many are the events that one would consider best forgotten.

Interest is the glue of memory.

MENACE

We live in a world of threats from nature and people, threats of pain and death.

The menace of death is never far from any person.

MENDING

Few things are there that cannot be mended.

One should constantly scrutinize one's ways and endeavour to mend what is defective.

MERIT

Merit alone does not determine success in life.

To be fair, merits and demerits should be considered together. All too often, in appraising a person, demerit has influenced us to forget his merits.

METHOD

Method is reason in the role of architect.

Where method is, simplicity and clarity reside.

MIDDLE

The middle is the position of mediocrity.

To steer a middle course is to be unenterprising.

MIGHT

The might of intellect triumphs over the might of brawn.

The might of a nation does not lie in its armed forces but in the greatness of its civilization.

MIMICRY

Mimicry is the lowest form of clowning.

Anything can be made to appear ludicrous by mimicry.

MIND

The mind is for thought, but thought is rare.

The body is the instrument of the mind.

It is surprising that people don't know their own minds when they are inside them.

A really open mind can belong only to an idiot. It contains no idea, and all that comes in goes out.

MIRROR

One reason for looking at a mirror in a car is to see whether a traffic policeman is following you!

MISANTHROPE

Misanthropes whose hatred does not extend beyond their minds are harmless.

MISER

Misers are not appreciated until after their death.

Misers suffer for the benefit of their heirs.

No one loves misers, and yet they have done no evil. They may have done no good either; but in a world where active evil works untold suffering, they deserve commendation than otherwise.

The miser lives a life of abstinence to accumulate what to others is a means for obtaining pleasure.

MIXTURE

Most things are a mixture of good and evil.

Some good things, when mixed with bad, cease to be good.

A mixture of truth and falsehood is a lie.

MOB

No mob can be good or right.

The same person behaves differently when he is an isolated individual and when he is a member of a mob. It is not only that he may follow the mob out of fear, but he acts as though his wits have temporarily deserted him and he has lost his identity.

The mob triumphs over individuals, however strong or wise they may be.

MOCKERY

The people have a strange capacity for making a mockery of a religion or ideology by not practising what they profess to believe.

To mock a person is the most insulting form of contempt.

MODERATION

Moderation is the characteristic of the mediocre.

Moderation works no havoc.

It would be preposterous not to pursue what is good to the full, if possible. Moderation is desirable only when excess is damaging and not otherwise.

MODERN

Much that is modern is refreshing and valueless.

Modernity is not synonymous with the truth and the right. What it does is to make life appear new and exhilarating.

What is modern is not necessarily new. It may be something revived or imported.

MOMENT

Human beings have but a moment of life, but that moment is brimful of meaning.

The moments of happiness are the gleaming jewels of memory.

A moment in popular parlance denotes an indefinite succession of moments.

MONEY

Money could be disregarded if the many things for which it stands were considered undesirable.

Most people would not consider their occupations sensible if they didn't make money.

Money occupies the central place in the mind of the average person.

The person in the street would prefer to make money than to know all about it.

To spend money is pleasant but to save it is pleasanter.

Many an ambitious project founders on the rock of funds.

Money is external and should not be taken into account in estimating a person's real worth.

MONOPOLY

In business, monopolies are prejudicial to the public. The principal defect of socialism is that a service becomes a monopoly, which is even more detrimental than a private monopoly, because it has no higher authority to oversee its operation.

MONUMENT

A monument without utility or aesthetic worth is a waste of public funds.

A monument is a tribute to vainglory or a propaganda stunt.

MOON

From the earth, people see the moon as a small circle of cold light with dark patches, but on this appearance they have reared a medley of fantasies. A sensory illusion is the fount of intellectual illusions.

The inconstant moon is the most glamorous denizen of the sky.

MORALE

If you want to win, you must not think you are in the wrong.

MORALITY

Morality can be of a kind which, clearly understood, is immorality.

Common morality is never more than a minimum standard of behaviour for social cohesion.

Formerly, morality condemned immorality; nowadays, immorality condemns morality.

MOTIVE

A right motive can inspire a wrong action.

Every crime must have a motive, but every motive need not issue in a crime.

A bad action with a bad motive is detestable; a bad action with a good motive is condemnable; a good action with a bad motive is deplorable; a good action with a good motive is admirable.

MUD

Evil is the mud of the mind.

Physical mud is not a pretty sight and one does not like to be defiled by it. Mental mud is uglier, and for one to be contaminated by it is much worse.

MUDDLE

Ordinary life has more muddle than method in its make-up.

MULTITUDE

An ideology that wins the multitude wins in the end.

The multitude is possessed of force but not intelligence; it is muscle, not brain.

MURDER

Murder is the biggest adder of crime.

A murder may never be discovered, but it will forever flap its dark wings in the cavern of the perpetrator's mind.

The habitual murderer is a monster out of the remote past.

A skilful murder is an expression of decadent art.

Murder is the associate of nightmares.

MUSEUM

A museum is history expressed in samples.

A museum is a treasure of objects, natural or artificial, whose influence on the extension of knowledge is immediate and powerful.

MUSIC

Music is emotional sound.

Music has charms to make the wild wilder.

Music everywhere and all the time has not produced greater composers and musicians or even better connoisseurs. It has only produced more irritability.

MYSTERY

Human beings love mystery because they luxuriate in the sensation of wonder.

A mystery can be thickened with the gravy of humbug.

N

NAÏVETÉ

Naïve is the person who believes a stranger when that stranger tells him that he has a scheme to benefit him.

If not for naïveté, deceivers would not be as successful as they are.

NAME

A name can by unwarranted association produce amusement that is puerile in character.

A famous name has its traducers and an infamous one its apologists.

A great name makes the commonplace interesting.

NARRATIVE

Narrative is more captivating than description.

A narrative without detail lacks colour; a narrative with an abundance of details lacks movement.

A true story is more appealing than fiction. When legends were created, they were popular because they were deemed reality.

NATIONALISM

If all groups in the world were treated as equal and would in actual fact suffer no disadvantage, nationalism would lose its appeal.

Nationalism is the worst manifestation of group selfishness.

An aggressor and his victim may both be fired by nationalism.

Nationalism is seen at its best when a people is trying to free itself from foreign oppression.

NATURE

Nature is best appreciated by the mind rather than the eye. The reflection over the sublimity of the immense universe greatly surpasses in value the enjoyment of the beauty of visible phenomena.

What is unnatural is often accounted natural.

Humankind is the only part of nature that can flout nature.

The indiscriminate love of nature, seeing nothing but goodness and beauty and ignoring the badness and ugliness, is not a sign of the nobility or sensitivity of a mind but if not an affectation, is evidence of wilful error.

The sun shines and the rain falls on all alike; nature does not discriminate between the good and the bad.

NECESSITY

A discovery or invention makes a necessity unnecessary.

Necessity is the scapegoat for many a wrong action.

Impelled by necessity, we can do things we never imagined we could.

Because a thing is a necessity, it doesn't follow that it is good; all that it necessitates is toleration.

NEED

One who needs little will be little in need.

Dire need leads to devious methods of alleviation.

The needy rich can never elicit any sympathy, and they are evidence of the limitlessness of human desire.

Food, water, and air are the only needs that cannot be eliminated.

The desk needs a chair. One thing needs another.

NEEDLE

The needle is the outdated symbol of the work of women.

The needle is such a tiny tool engaged in such excessive toil.

NEGATIVE

To be able to say no is necessary if one wants to be a revolutionary.

The negative may be the positive viewed from the opposite side.

NEGLIGENCE

Negligence is laxity regarded as a fault or crime.

Negligence can be due to laziness or haste, and it is seldom justifiable, though it is not human nature to be careful at all times.

A little neglect can breed serious consequences out of all proportion to the fault.

NEIGHBOUR

Neighbours make the best friends and the worst enemies.

A neighbour contributes to one's happiness or misery.

Fretting yourself to death trying to do what your neighbour does shows the folly of imitation.

NERVE

A weak body does not preclude a strong nerve.

NEST

Every bird has a nest but not every person a house. This does not speak well of human superiority.

A nest is the symbol of a cosy home.

NET

The net has caught the fish. The plan has produced money.

A net stands as the symbol of system.

NEUTRALITY

Neutrality is seldom strict; it tends to lean to one side—benevolent neutrality to one and malevolent neutrality to the other.

What's wrong with sitting on the fence? The ground on either side may be muddy.

To be neutral merely to avoid a duty is a transgression.

Neutrality is impartiality, but this could be indifference to, regard for, or opposition of both sides.

NEVER

"Never" is a difficult word to substantiate.

No one has ever never done wrong—or right.

Never has anyone seen so much and done so little as the tourist.

NEW YEAR

There's little reason to celebrate the New Year, for it is seldom better than the old.

Naïve hope blooms brightest at the New Year.

NEWNESS

Much of what we call new is the old revived.

One who practises what is new suffers vilification; one who sticks to what has gone out of date is a laughingstock; one who follows what has become fashionable avoids the penalties of both extremes and enjoys the grandeur of being a member of the vulgar crowd.

NEWS

What is news? Tittle-tattle, scandal, and crime. It is less harrowing to be present at a catastrophe than to await the news thereof.

It is amazing that a reporter can be kept so busy, as there are so few things worth reporting.

Bitter news does not travel to a sweet reception.

The stranger the event, the more enamouring the news.

NICHE

Every person has his little niche in the world. Those of the great and the little do not differ much in real value but differ frightfully in human estimation.

NIGHT

Night is the time for thought.

The peace of night is welcome after the unrest of day.

Humans make night hideous by using it as a cover for the commission of foul crime.

NIGHTMARE

It is unfortunate that even in sleep one could suffer terror—the terror of nightmares.

NOISE

Noise begets attention.

Noise is irritating, and silence is oppressive.

The noise of a quarrel never fails to draw eager listeners. Not all noises are unpleasant, and apparently the pleasantest is that of discord!

The noise of machinery does not exist in nature; it is the tuneless tune of industrial civilization.

NONSENSE

Nonsense makes the most hilarious jokes.

No nonsense but has its advocates.

What is sense to one person is nonsense to another.

A solemn person uttering solemn nonsense is the most ludicrous of spectacles.

NOON

Noon divides the day into two equal parts with its seal of heat.

Noon is as garish and unpleasant as midnight is soft and soothing.

NORMALITY

To be normal is the ideal of the person in the street and the psychologist.

The normal is not necessarily the right.

To be normal is to be mediocre.

What is normal in one society is abnormal in another.

NOTHING

Something can contain nothing; but nothing, save space, can contain something.

One who does nothing is nothing.

Nothing is to be preferred to a thing that is pernicious.

The nihilist believes in nothing; the indigent has nothing; the indolent does nothing; nothing remains forever.

One who has nothing to think and nothing to do should vanish into nothing.

It is surprising what a multitude of things said and done mean nothing.

NOVEL

The novel is the biography of the ordinary person.

NUDITY

Nudity in public would cause no embarrassment, shame, amusement, curiosity, or horror if it were common. But there is no advantage in having it.

Nudism is group nakedness, a ridiculous reversion to the practice of prehistoric times.

NUISANCE

A fly is a nuisance; so is one who never leaves off one's favourite subject.

Nuisances are of many varieties, ranging from a heap of rubbish to a drunk. Some can be eliminated, while others have to be tolerated.

Life at times seems to be a nuisance.

Irritability finds everything a nuisance.

NUMBER

Number is the bed of mathematics.

A number is methodical for identifying a person or thing, but a name is soothing. The difference between name and number is the difference between art and science.

Numbering is the sister of systematization.

A big number is always imposing.

O

OATH

An oath is a call on superstition to reinforce a statement.

If people intend to deceive, an oath will not bind them.

OBEDIENCE

Obedience is not a virtue but is merely a device for action.

Obedience is the child of fear.

Obedience is the tool of the tyrant.

OBLIGATION

It does most good to repay an obligation when the other party is in need of help.

To be under an obligation is to be in debt.

Be slow to incur an obligation.

People are not compelled to do kind deeds, but they are obliged by virtue of their humanity to do so.

Obligation is sister to gratitude.

To perform a service, not out of kindness but to put a person under an obligation for the purpose of future exploitation, is not a meritorious act.

OBLIVION

Oblivion of a tragedy is not the best course; quiet remembrance is better.

Oblivion has the unpleasant sweetness of flight from a difficult situation that should be fought and overcome.

OBSCURITY

Obscurity is obscurity and cannot paradoxically confer light. The mystic does not glimpse the truth.

Obscurity of meaning does not make writing profound but only shows that the author is pretending to knowledge he does not possess or has cobwebs over his understanding.

OBSTACLE

An obstacle provokes a determined person to greater action but cows a weak person to extinction.

OBSTINACY

Obstinacy is persistence in what offends us!

When the less one understands and the more one argues, one's obstinacy is apparent.

A person who will not budge an inch when a volcano is brewing will be engulfed by the lava.

Obstinate people are very exasperating because they won't yield to our obstinate insistence!

Obstinacy may turn out right or wrong. If it turns out right, the firmness is justified, and if it turns out wrong, the folly is apparent.

People who are obstinate in everything they believe are either given to exhaustive reflection or to conceit.

OCCUPATION

Specialization is good for skill but not for intellectual character.

People who so identify themselves with their occupation that in respect of intellectual qualities and moral traits they are typical of what their colleagues are supposed to be, forfeit their worth as individual human beings.

An occupation is the shell, not the kernel, of life.

An occupation is merely a means of earning a living, and to identify a person with it is ludicrous.

Every occupation has its use or society would not pay for the work performed, but its worth is not to be judged by the amount of money earned.

OCEAN

The ocean is not the friend of humankind.

Water occupies nearly three-fourths of the surface of the globe; if human beings could explore the land below the oceans as thoroughly as they do dry land, what treasures it would reveal!

To be tossed in a ship in the middle of an ocean is to realize how puny humankind is.

OFFENCE

Not to give offence at all is strange, for anything can give offence to someone.

Be wary of giving offence and be slow to take it.

OFFICE

An office gives a nincompoop an imposing appearance.

An office is just a job, and it should be judged as such and in no other light.

The incompetence, waste, and corruption of public office throughout history is sufficient to condemn socialism.

OIL

Oil floats on water. The frivolous element in a society is supported by the earnest section.

Oil reduces friction between two moving surfaces. Persuasion decreases disharmony between two conflicting parties.

OMEN

There are no omens; there are only false beliefs.

Reliance on omens is the last resort of ignorance.

An omen is a peril, as it makes for certainty where none exists and leads to foolhardy action.

OPINION

The opinion of the public is not more likely to be true than the opinion of the individual.

The opinion of society commences as the opinion of one person.

Opinion is not synonymous with truth.

It is the mark of a rational person to arrive at an opinion after due deliberation and yet to be able to change it when fresh considerations arise.

Harmony ensues if my opinion is yours and your opinion is mine!

The ordinary person's opinions are guided by feeling rather than by fact.

OPPORTUNITY

When one opportunity is missed, look for another. It's rare that anything occurs only once.

When an opportunity occurs, it should be taken and no needless difficulties raised.

Prepare yourself, or you will not be able to utilize the opportunity that springs into sight.

OPPOSITION

Opposition for opposition's sake is the canker of democracy.

Opposition increases the energy of the resolute.

People have a tendency to form opposing groups on every issue.

When anybody proposes a new idea, the first reaction is opposition.

No government can ever have unanimous support. When force is used to achieve this, all that happens is that the opposition is driven underground and works insidiously.

OPPRESSION

The person in power tends to exercise oppression in great or small measure. It's human to demonstrate one's prowess.

Slavery is the direst form of oppression.

Oppression is evil, whether legal or illegal.

OPTIMISM

An optimist refuses to see the worm in the bud.

Optimism is hope beyond hope.

There is a bright side to everything, provided it materializes.

Optimists think that luck is always on their side; pessimists, that it is always against them.

ORATORY

Oratory is a mellifluous flow of language with reason puffing a few breaths in the background.

A popular orator is a person who discourses at great length on commonplace topics, employing a minimum of thought and no originality to persuade or keep his audience to a certain point of view.

ORDER

Order is the dictator's slogan. But the dictator must be the person to impose it, and the result is inharmonious order.

Order is needed in thought as in action.

Everything starts off in chaos, from which order has to be evolved.

ORDINARY

What is ordinary is comfortable.

The ordinary causes no surprise.

Ordinary life is humdrum but not free of trouble.

The ordinary person grew in importance with democracy and socialism but will suffer a relapse if absolutism persists for long.

The extraordinary person is ordinary in everything, save that in respect of which he is noted.

ORGANIZATION

Systematic organization is the manufacturer of efficiency.

Organization for organization's sake is quixotic if no purpose is served thereby.

Organization of one's time and work will produce the best results.

ORIGIN

Origin is not synonymous with worth.

The secret of the origin of a phenomenon is usually encased in a strong box.

If we want to know a thing thoroughly, we must also study its origin and its history.

ORIGINALITY

Originality is genius.

True originality seldom succeeds.

Because originality has come to be deemed commendable, many a celebrity is lauded as original when he is nothing of the sort.

When critics come across something original, they dislike it because it is queer; when they see something ordinary, they dislike it because it is trite.

ORNAMENT

Judicious ornament adds beauty to beauty.

Garish ornamentation is artificial and depressing.

The flower is the ornament of nature.

ORTHODOXY

One who can't think is orthodox.

OWNERSHIP

The joy of ownership is a profound feeling.

One who owns little and that of little value could not be more careful were it a treasure.

No possession is better than knowledge.

P

PAIN

Pain has a meaning deeper than pleasure. It is an urgent signal of disorder that requires rectification. To bear it because it is deemed good is ridiculous. The first duty of humankind is to eliminate it as much as possible. To inflict it on others is crime and on oneself folly. To be able to endure it bravely is stoicism, commendable when unavoidable.

To find pleasure in pain is appropriate only in art.

Pain may be ephemeral, but its memory has a long life.

Pain engenders thought.

PAINT

Paint makes a gay appearance but a wall remains the same. The look is only the look of the paint.

PANIC

When panic springs in, reason bolts off.

Mob panic is exponentially worse than individual panic.

Panic is fear grown crazy.

Panic never solves a problem.

Those who always use reason will not panic and belie their nature.

PARALLELNESS

Lines may run parallel, but nothing else does.

PARK

A park is an artificial slice of countryside in a town.

An overcrowded park is a civic area with trees.

The attraction of a park flows from its beauty, serenity, freshness, and freedom.

PARODY

A parody is an imitation concocted of spite and ignorance.

The humour of a parody is of a low kind, and it requires little skill to produce.

Anything, the best and the worst, can be parodied.

PART

The part is superior to the whole.

Humankind is the most significant part of the scheme of things and must fulfil its role worthily.

To take risks when one stands to lose only a part of one's fortune shows a combination of prudence and adventurousness.

PARTIALITY

When one likes a person, his faults are merits; when one dislikes him, they are atrocities.

Partiality is kinsman to prejudice.

PARTNER

In business, one is more likely to be cheated by a partner than by anybody else.

It requires generosity to be an ungrumbling partner. As it is difficult for partners to make absolutely equal contributions to an enterprise, and still more difficult for one not to fancy that his contribution is more important, a partnership engenders considerable dissatisfaction.

PARTY

Two kinds of people can be dangerous to a leader: the first are those outside his party and the second those in his party.

There is no reason for people to be brigands, for they can always join a political party.

Most of the members of a party are in it for trifling gains, and when they see it is unpopular and no benefit is likely to accrue to them, they forsake it and join another.

PASSION

The stronger the passion, the weaker the reason.

Passion is the director of human action.

Passion run rampant is a destructive force.

Hatred is a stronger passion than love.

PASTIME

Angling may be a pastime for the person but it is not a pastime for the fish.

Time is so valuable that it is preferable that even a pastime should possess some utility.

PATIENCE

Patience is unpleasant but is often necessary.

One who is patient may eventually attain what one wants or may sit and wait forever. Patience in itself means little.

Standing in a queue is the best way to learn patience.

Patience is the passive hope of eventual success.

Patience is not a virtue but merely a procedure not always desirable.

PEACE

Peace has numerous arts; war has but one.

Peace begins in the mind.

Peace is not always fair, but it is never evil.

War as an instrument of peace is a contradiction in terms and an absurdity in theory and practice.

Oppressive peace is not desirable peace.

PEARL

An oyster is badly maltreated. Its flesh is eaten and its pearl is taken away. This is a clear case of adding insult to injury!

Pearls are doubly enclosed in an oyster in the sea.

PEN

A pistol made of a pen to liquidate misconceptions and abuses is the only right pistol.

The pen is the weapon of the brain.

Writers should sterilize their pens from the germs of evil.

PEOPLE

Nothing is more dishonest than the habit of politicians and dictators of declaring what the people want, meaning thereby what they themselves want.

The people may not know the right means and ends, but they receive the consequences.

The people are not a homogeneous entity but consist of the wise and the foolish, the good and the wicked, of thinkers, artists, lawyers, merchants, workers, and peasants. It is erroneous to refer to the people admiringly or contemptuously, as though possessed of one mind.

PERFECTION

Nothing in the world is perfect, but it is possible to arrive nearer to perfection.

Perfection may just be the attainment of an imperfect ideal.

PERFORMANCE

Performance always falls short of expectation, and this is rightly so, or stagnation will result.

An endeavour should be made to perform every task with the utmost efficiency and dispatch.

People judge others by their own performance.

Many a performance would be better unperformed.

PERMANENCE

Nothing under the sun is permanent.

PERSECUTION

Unremitting persecution is the trademark of tyranny.

Persecution can always discover an excuse. The saddest thing is to find the press of a country expatiating on the necessity and beauty of the policies of a persecuting government.

Persecution breeds retaliation, and the more violence it displays, the more violence it evokes.

The essence of persecution is the maintenance of power and privilege; all else is camouflage.

PERSEVERANCE

Persist if you think fit; desist if you think futile.

Nothing needs perseverance more than original work.

Perseverance, like so many other things, depends on results for its assessment. If it leads to nothing or to disaster, it is condemned; if to success, lauded.

PERSONALITY

Personality influences success, and success influences personality.

Personality is not as significant as it is generally presumed to be. It is naïve to consider that every eminent person has an outstanding personality and every nonentity no personality.

Many roads lead to success, and it is gratuitous to assume that charisma is the attribute of every great national leader.

PERSUASION

Persuasion is a skill unrelated to truth.

The vulgar are apt to mistake mass persuasion for truth.

Orators and advocates are judged by their persuasive power, which does not necessarily denote high intelligence.

PESSIMISM

The pessimist believes that whatever glitters is not gold.

Pessimism is joy in misery.

As viewed by the pessimist, the world can only remain stationary or get worse.

PETAL

A petal is the most beautiful part of a plant and the least useful. Beauty is not utility; it is just beauty.

The brilliant-hued petals of a flower set in a calyx of green sepals constitute a dream of delight.

PHILANTHROPY

Philanthropy gilds knavery.

Philanthropists attract many an application to dip into their kindness and purse.

Philanthropy is the aspirin of society; it relieves but does not cure ills.

It is profitable philanthropy to rob a bank and denote the petty cash to some worthy cause!

PHILOSOPHY

Philosophy is the chairman of the society of knowledge.

The worst kind of philosopher is one who sets out to rationalize the deeds of a person of action and weave a system out of his ideas.

PICTURE

A picture is a description in great detail.

Because the camera could instantaneously make a completely accurate representation, painters took to making inaccurate representations to overcome a rival.

PITY

Pity should be felt, not spoken.

The pitiless person in triumph need expect no pity in defeat.

Pity is sorrow at the sorrow of others and is the noblest form of human sympathy.

PLACE

That place should differ from place is but right.

People in high place are not cognizant of people in low place, though they may dwell in the same place.

PLAN

No plan is so faultless that it can never fail.

A plan, however superb, does not stand the test of time.

PLATITUDE

It is not right to despise or violate a platitude if it were the truth. But many platitudes are really erroneous, and they should be condemned on this account and not because they are commonplace.

People affect to despise platitudes, though they are in reality enmeshed in them. What they designate platitudes are commonplace ideas that have gone out of fashion; what they follow are the current ideas, which they do not call platitudes.

PLAY

To treat play more seriously than work is symptomatic of an effete civilization.

All play and no work appears to be the modern ideal.

PLEASING

Favour acquired purely by pleasing is precarious.

The art of pleasing verges dangerously on the art of flattery.

Few things are pleasing forever.

It is good to please wherever possible; it is expedient to displease wherever needed.

PLOTTING

The balloon of plotting has never yet been devised that cannot be punctured.

Plotting may be good or evil according to its objective.

POETRY

Poetry is emotion in a striking web of words.

Nothing sticks to the memory like a poem. Even after the lapse of years, it still remains as scintillating as ever. One is tempted to believe that there exists a special affinity between memory and poetry.

Poetry is an intellectual intoxicant.

Poetry would not be significant if it were not steeped in profound thought.

Great poetry is the best distillation of thought and language.

The province of poetry is the universe.

POLITENESS

Politeness is often mendacity to avoid hurt.

Excessive politeness is a bore.

POLITICS

The good party person is devoid of thought.

The usual political party consists of a collection of nincompoops intent on achieving a nefarious purpose.

Politics is not morals, but the state should promote a minimum morality, that which prevents one person from injuring another.

The logic of politicians is that, if the other person is a villain, they themselves must *ipso facto* be heroes, and if they do the opposite of what the other does, their actions automatically become right.

One who plays with a ball is a sportsman; one who plays with stocks and shares is a speculator; one who plays with the happiness of the people is a politician.

The politician lives on promises that sound pleasant until their fulfilment is overdue.

A full-grown voice and a half-grown brain are good for a political career.

Politicians are never selfish; they work devotedly for the welfare of the people, provided they are in power and enjoy the perks of office.

Politics brings out the worst of human nature.

POPULARITY

Popularity is the least reliable of all commodities.

Popularity is not all admiration; it begets jealousy and vilification, at least on the part of a section of the populace.

One should do what one wants to do primarily for its own sake; popularity is a secondary consideration.

Popularity denotes success but not necessarily worth.

POPULATION

The population explosion, if it continues on and on, will be worse than the nuclear bomb for exploding society.

It is strange that we should feel depressed that the world may contain more human beings than animals.

Were the world one state, population could be more evenly distributed around the globe.

POSITIVE

What has being is positive, but it may be either good or bad.

It is better to have negative good than positive evil.

POSSIBILITY

Many impossible things are possible, but that does not mean that anything is possible.

Constructing possibility as probability leads to many a catastrophe.

If one is determined on a certain achievement, the possibility of failure should only lurk dimly in the background.

POSTERITY

The fate of posterity hinges on the events of present times.

It's a shame for governments to saddle posterity with the debts they incur.

In improving the quality of our life, we'll be ameliorating the welfare of posterity.

POTENTIALITY

Others are not interested in our potentialities.

The potential good should be developed and the potential evil eradicated.

What is potential need not necessarily come to fruition. Work and chance are important factors in its promotion.

POVERTY

Poverty is born with humankind, but with progress, it can be eradicated.

The poverty of the individual is the disgrace of society.

Misery not associated with poverty tends to wear an air of unreality.

POWER

Power for power's sake is the craze of the dictator, and nothing can be worse.

One who has risen to power from a low position is no less ferocious than one who is born to power.

A sentiment expressed when one is in power looks ludicrous when one is in defeat, and pitiable is the person who makes the turnabout.

No person would have sufficient power to rule a people if it did not succumb psychologically.

Success, not succession, is the way of the modern autocrat.

Respect for authority is defeat in mind as well as in fact.

PRACTICE

Practice should fit snugly the mould of theory.

Practice without regard to the good is objectionable.

It is better to be unpractical than to be the practical person whose practice is villainous.

The truth of a principle that is not practised is not invalidated thereby.

PRAISE

When one bestows praise, it is for qualities one likes; if one possesses the same quality, praise of another person is in effect self-praise.

Praise proportionate to worth is the correct procedure, but it is rarely seen.

No fan blows such a soothing breeze as praise.

There are three types of praise: great praise, small praise, and no praise.

PRAYER

Prayer is solicitation of free benefits.

Prayers answered are made much of; those unanswered are conveniently forgotten.

PRECEDENT

A precedent is not a justification for a similar action, for two sets of circumstances are not identical or it might have been wrongly made. But it is commonly cited as though it were a sufficient reason.

PREDICTION

The anxious mind seeks predictions.

Having one's fortune told fills one with hope and disappointment.

There will always be people bent on foretelling the future and people to believe them. There is no better example of the credulity that never dies.

When the prediction of one soothsayer turns out right and that of another wrong, it is not a question of cleverness but luck, for one guess is no more reliable than the other.

Economic prophecies are about as reliable as weather forecasts.

PREJUDICE

Prejudice makes of the mind a locked box with the key lost.

Prejudice is irrational and at variance with truth.

To act in accordance with prejudice is unhappily the common practice.

Prejudice runs parallel to folly.

Nobody has any prejudices; everybody holds only truths!

PREPARATION

Preparation for action is not essential, but it doubles its effectiveness.

In any course of action, one should be prepared against contingencies and difficulties.

Preparation should just be adequate for its purpose; too much is as undesirable as too little.

PRETENCE

Pretending to be what one is not is the outcome of social life.

Pretence is the child of incompetence.

When pretence puts on its mask, truth totters in the mind.

From playful pretence to criminal deceit is an easy transition.

PREVENTION

To prevent a crime is more meritorious than to arrest a criminal.

To prevent repetition of a fault, make a strong resolution and persistently keep it in mind.

PRICE

Price is what the buyer likes to reduce and the seller to increase.

When prices go up, our hearts go down.

PRIDE

Pride does not injure others but exasperates.

Pride should be offensive only if mixed with contempt.

Pride is ridiculous, considering the pettiness of the things of which one is commonly proud.

PRINCIPLE

Principle before practice.

The person without principles is to be found in politics more than in any other sphere of activities. This is the most disastrous of tragedies, for it is the state that determines the quality of the life of the people.

A good principle unrealized is preferable to an evil practice triumphant.

Sincerity in thought and practice does not make a principle true.

PROBABILITY

Probability is the criterion of truth. It is all we can expect, for we have no faculty and no method to ensure that a belief cannot be wrong.

PROBLEMS

Problems accompany us more than our shadows.

Different countries and different ages have to tackle problems that are basically similar and have no final solution.

The greatest problem of all time is the universe.

PROGRESS

Reviving a barbaric practice is not progress.

Progress is triumphant change in the right direction.

To stand still is seldom desirable; to go forward is generally right.

Humankind has never been a stranger to progress.

Progress is a zigzag line.

PROMISE

One should not make a promise without knowing what it is all about beforehand.

Promises should not be lightly made, for they should be strongly kept.

A person who makes too many promises is not to be trusted.

It is dangerous to rely on promises.

A promise made under one set of circumstances looks different under another.

PROOF

A genuine proof is difficult to come by, while a specious proof can always be adduced.

Appeal to authority is not proof of truth.

Popularity proves nothing.

Orators do not persuade their audience by resorting to irrefragable proofs.

PROPAGANDA

Propaganda is public lying for a public purpose.

If individuals spin a false tale, they are stigmatized as liars; if a government publishes a series of romantic distortions, it is doing its duty.

Propaganda is the sister of advertisement.

PROPENSITY

Human propensities are difficult to change; their manifestations in action depend on the force of circumstances.

A propensity to do good is not the characteristic of the average person.

PROPERTY

There is nothing wrong with property per se. Capitalist property is iniquitous, not because it is private property but because it is unjustly acquired.

People love their possessions and rarely give them up unless constrained to do so.

Property is for people, not people for property.

Common property is nobody's property.

Nobody cares to own a desert. Property is coveted for its use.

PROSE

Prose need not necessarily be prosaic, while a lot of poetry, especially the modern kind, is worse than prosaic.

All language is artificial, and it is irrational to consider as natural the prose ordinarily spoken or written and to condemn as artificial unusual prose.

PROSPERITY

Prosperity is hard to acquire and easy to lose.

Unremitting prosperity is as wearisome as unrelieved adversity is tragic.

Prosperity after a hard struggle is meritorious; prosperity without any struggle is luck; prosperity as a consequence of evil is accursed.

PRUDENCE

Prudence prevents great loss and great gain.

Too much prudence will make for irresolution and ineffectualness in this uncertain world.

Prudence is the foe of adventure.

Prudence extends to details.

Without prudence, a genius can face ruin.

PUBLIC

The public has no mind of its own; it follows convention, obeys government, and shouts with demagogues.

The public has no right to trample over the individual.

The public lives, thinks, and acts on repute. Whatever has acquired a name is what it supports.

PUBLIC LIFE

Constant attendance at meetings makes many a mediocre person achieve success in public life.

PUNCTUALITY

To wait is hard; to arrive on time is easy.

The watch is the companion of punctuality.

Punctuality is always right, for if the other person is unpunctual, he is in the wrong.

PUNISHMENT

The severer the punishment, the more heinous crime becomes.

For justice, punishment should be equal to the crime; for humanity, it could well be less.

The aims of punishment are to promote justice, to make it serve as a deterrent, and to reform the wrong-doer. It is as misleading for it to be dangerously lenient as for it to be inordinately severe.

Punishment that is beyond endurance is monstrous.

PURCHASE

Buying on the instalment plan is lengthening the agony of payment.

Before purchasing a necessity, be sure that it is a necessity if your aim is not to give yourself an excuse for spending money you can ill afford to spend.

The treatment of the customer varies according to the general state of business.

PURITY

Purity should recognize impurity to avoid defilement.

PURPOSE

Purpose shapes action.

A strong purpose can make a person endure drastic privations.

An institution that does not fulfil its purpose should be discarded.

Q

QUALITY

Quality enchants; quantity astounds.

The quality of the mind determines a person's worth.

No quality should be deemed so important that all others are considered insignificant.

A pleasing quality may be unpleasing at times.

QUARREL

A quarrel that may begin with a fault on one side ends, if prolonged, with faults on both sides.

When three or more persons enter into a quarrel, they eventually settle down to form two opposing sides.

A quarrel must needs leave one disquieted

QUESTIONING

It's easy to ask questions but difficult to answer them.

Unanswerable questions are all round us.

Socrates was killed because he asked too many questions.

QUEUE

The queue is the indicator of population outstripping service.

QUIBBLING

The quibbler is not a lover of truth.

Quibbling is the last resort of the loser.

QUIXOTRY

To entrust a thief with your property is quixotic.

Quixotic behaviour makes pleasant reading but unpleasant reality.

R

RACE

The differences among the diverse races are slight, but national arrogance exaggerates them.

Pride of race is the most irrational and aggressive of all forms of pride.

RAIN

Rain is refreshing, but few welcome it at any one time.

Nature, the gardener, waters the earth with rain but in uneven quantities.

Things are so interrelated that, if there were no rain, all land would be a desert, and it would harbour no life.

RAINBOW

A rainbow is a dream in the sky.

RARENESS

To be rare is to be valuable. This is the way people evaluate worth, though it is faulty. In reality, what is common often holds greater worth.

RASHNESS

Rashness is the prelude to ruin.

Sometimes one has to throw caution to the winds and embark on a course of action seemingly rash, but this is deliberate adventure and not thoughtless hastiness.

RATIONING

Where there is rationing, a black market whispers into existence.

Rationing is the smell of a straitened economy.

READING

Reading is the best of pastimes, if only because of the variety of its fare.

Reading is vicarious experience.

One who does not read cannot possess much knowledge of humankind and nature.

If one reads for recreation, one's judgment can be suspended; if one reads for knowledge, one's critical faculties should be on the *qui vive*.

REALITY

Tackling reality will bring greater gain than harbouring illusion.

Reality is an elusive elf.

Reality is sometimes pleasant, sometimes horrible. We have to take it as it is and mould it as much as possible for our welfare.

REASON

Every person can reason, but few do so.

We reject reason, and truth rejects us.

Reason takes no account of popularity; one hundred million people can be wrong.

One reason puts ten fancies to flight.

Reason of a specious kind can be found to buttress any argument.

There are two categories of persons who will not reason: they are the obstinate, who insist on sticking to their prejudices, and the accommodating, who believe what other people believe and do not consider that minority opinion can ever be right.

REBELLION

A government gets the rebellion it deserves.

Rebellion is anathema to a government, but that does not make it bad.

The justification of a rebellion resides in the circumstances.

Rebellion is a traumatic event and is to be condemned if undertaken for ambition or on trifling grounds.

REBUKE

Rebuke, however well deserved, is never appreciated.

A rebuke in public cuts twice as deeply as a rebuke in private.

A silent rebuke in the form of a look or an example engenders consternation and not resentment.

RECIPROCITY

There are two aspects to treatment; they are not to injure others and not to be injured by others.

Reciprocal treatment holds the greatest sense and satisfaction.

Reciprocity does not necessarily signify virtue, for two persons may support each other in doing evil.

The average person does not yearn for you to do to him as you would that he does to you, but prefers you to do for him what he wants.

When a person enters the sea, which is not his natural abode, and gets eaten by a shark, it is considered evil; but if he kills it instead, he is considered heroic.

RECONCILIATION

Reconciliation is a sweet as enmity is bitter.

One who is not too proud to take the first step in effecting reconciliation will have hardly any enemies.

The longer dissension lasts, the more difficult the reconciliation.

REDUNDANCY

Nothing is more humiliating to an employee than to find that he is considered redundant.

The economically minded does not own anything redundant.

What is redundant for our purpose should not be thrown away, for it may be needed on another occasion.

Redundancy in the use of words is a waste.

REFORM

Reform is the desire of distress out to annihilate itself.

A reform aimed at removing a few glaring abuses is like patching a coat, which would become more serviceable but would still be a defective garment.

REGRET

We go through life with our mind a museum of regrets.

We may regret having performed an action or we may regret not having done so. Regret has no fixed direction.

A kind action should entail no regret, though the recipient turns out to be ungrateful.

RELATIVE

Grumbling against relatives is the fruit of disappointed expectations.

Help from a relative is less appreciated than help from a stranger because it is taken for granted.

Dislike of a man should not extend to his son.

Most distant relatives are near strangers.

People will not do for their relatives what they will do for their boss.

RELIGION

Those who say all religions are equally true are not displaying their broad-mindedness but their indifference.

The reason people talk of religion shamefacedly is because they don't practise their own.

Religion nowadays resembles the ruin of a stately edifice sentimentally cherished for its historical associations.

REMEDY

A remedy should just tally with the complaint.

No person can remedy a person's defects and disappointments, save himself.

The more perilous the situation, the more drastic the remedy.

The same remedy does not work for every apparently similar situation.

REMORSE

Remorse is self-inflicted revenge.

The wish that something shouldn't have happened is the vainest and bitterest of all wishes.

Remorse without restitution in the fullest measure possible is a mere idle gnawing of the conscience.

REPETITION

Repetition of the same food at successive meals makes for nausea; repetition of the same remarks at frequent intervals makes for exasperation.

REPLACEMENT

People are not as important as they think. There is always someone who can do another's work.

In replacing a missing article, it is preferable to have one slightly better unless on grounds of harmony an identical one is sought.

Careful use makes for few replacements.

REPRESENTATION

Representation is the art of presenting different aspects to different people.

The ordinary representative is an ordinary person.

Too often elected representatives become the representative of themselves only.

Representatives are elected by the electorate on the things they propose to do, but they behave as though they were elected to do anything they like.

The voters elect those they support, but the elected do not support those who elect them.

Voters are commonly faced with the problem of having to decide which of the candidates put forward is the least objectionable.

The electorate may know that their representative is a fool or a villain, but they would still elect him rather than the wise and virtuous because he resembles them.

REPUBLIC

Few are the republics that have worked for the good of the public.

A republic can be as tyrannical as a monarchy.

Republics where the welfare of all the people is not promoted and from which freedom is absent are travesties.

RESENTMENT

Resentment over injustice rankles deep and long.

One easily resents criticism but as easily forgets it.

RESIGNATION

Resignation is a poor refuge.

One may have to yield to the inevitable, but far too often the difficult is mistaken for the inevitable.

RESOLUTION

Resolutions are not made to be kept. Everybody makes resolutions to change for the better, but success is rare.

Consider what you have to do, resolve to do it, and do it.

Don't make resolutions only at the New Year, for they are the least successful.

RESOURCES

One day the earth's resources will vanish and humankind will have none left. That is a frightful thought, but most people would assert that there is no need for us to agonize over it, as we can leave posterity to look after its own affairs.

RESPECT

Genuine respect cannot be forced.

More than any other quality, respect has to be mutual; if you don't respect others, they will not respect you.

One who desires respect must earn it.

RESPONSIBILITY

Success needs the ability to gauge responsibility and the courage to shoulder it.

It is not right that a job should have no real work but have only responsibility.

Responsibility means that one person does wrong and another bears the blame.

REST

Rest is the sister of sleep.

Too much rest is sloth; too little, suicide.

Rest is as indispensable for the mind as for the body.

RESULT

Every action has its result.

Result is the judge of worth.

RETREAT

No army retreats if it can win on the spot.

A strategic retreat is at best a tactical defeat.

REVENGE

Revenge is justice that the law has failed to execute, refuses to execute, or is waiting to execute.

If it were not for fear of revenge, the evil-doer would perpetrate even greater misdeeds.

Revenge is not a delicious food but a bitter drug.

REVERIE

A reverie is a pleasant pastime that may generate fresh ideas.

Addiction to reverie is the foe of success in practical life.

A reverie is a dream with the mind in a conscious state.

REVOLUTION

A violent revolution is less destructive than a war.

Revolution is thought in stormy action.

Systematic destruction and systematic construction should be the two complementary facets of revolution.

A revolution is not wrong per se, for no government has a sacred right to rule.

No one needs to succeed more than revolutionaries, for their heroism or villainy depends on the outcome of their struggle.

A revolution has its origin in thinkers, is spread by people of action, and explodes with the masses.

REWARD

Reward is the complement of punishment, and it should go with it.

A reward not commensurate with the task deters further enterprise.

One who does good without seeking rewards is the most truly good.

It is better to reward than to punish.

To avoid dissatisfaction and unhappiness, think more of the rewards you have received than of those you have missed.

RIDDLE

Riddles are queer things; to remain riddles, they must not be solved, yet their *raison d'être* is to be solved.

Human knowledge is the accumulation of the results of the arduous solution of riddles.

RIDICULE

We flush with embarrassment when we feel we are ridiculous; we flush with anger when we are objects of ridicule.

Ridicule can be the weapon of the fool as well as the wit.

Ridicule does not prove that a thing is right or wrong.

RIGHT

Rightness does not confer the right to trample on the wrong.

A ripe fruit is right for us and for the plant; if we follow nature, we are never wrong.

Proving your opponent wrong doesn't prove that you are right.

Right does not make might any more than might makes right.

To do right may not be difficult, but to continue doing it certainly is.

RISK

An army that does not take risks has no chance of winning.

RIVER

What is the object of the river? It conveys fresh water to the sea to be made impure!

Rivers may be large or small, straight or sinuous, swift or slow, placid or turbulent, murmuring or thunderous; whatever they may be, they are of all waters the most useful to humankind and the most delightful to behold, and their ceaseless motion makes them seem alive.

ROAD

The air has no road and innumerable roads.

The steep, winding road wears a menacing look on a picturesque face.

ROMANCE

Romance is a luxury derived from gazing at the Milky Way of unreality.

The tragedy of romance is not that it portrays a dream world but that the world it depicts is believed to be in accordance with reality. Its greater tragedy is that its values and its ideas of the desirable and sublime are puerile.

RUIN

If you wish to avoid ruin, ponder carefully over everything you do.

Ruin can come from inside as from outside a person.

The modern age does not prize ancient ideas but values the ruins of ancient artefacts.

RULE

Strict adherence to a rule will eventually bring disaster.

A new rule is as apt to engender aversion and opposition as a *nouveau riche*.

No rule has no exceptions.

There are far too many rules in all spheres of human activity; they should be reduced to a minimum.

RUMOUR

A rumour has its origin in one person who has effaced himself.

Rumour does not maintain a constant shape.

The tongue of rumour is tipped with poison.

A rumour is not necessarily total untruth. It is as unwise to reject it categorically as to swallow it whole. One should give it some thought and arrive at one's own conclusion.

S

SAFETY

Our entire life, from beginning to end, is unsafe.

It is more unsafe to tread a city street than a jungle path.

An aeroplane may crash through the roof and kill a person in his bed.

SAINT

The sinner turned saint has the best of both worlds.

Saintliness that is preoccupied with suffering and death is morbid and has no useful place in life.

SALESMANSHIP

Salesmanship is the art of persuading people to buy what they don't want.

Salesmanship is the cousin of advertising.

Salesmanship requires patience, politeness, garrulity, and a terribly thick skin.

SAMPLE

Goods supplied are never better than the sample and are frequently worse.

Nobody is more conscious of family than the sample; it proclaims that all the members of its family possess the same superb qualities.

SARCASM

Sarcasm makes pleasant literary reading but unpleasant social relationships.

Sarcasm has more sting than humour. It is a species of ridicule and insult.

SATIETY

Satiety spells ennui.

Appetite should be controlled at a point below satiety.

SATISFACTION

In human affairs, do not expect too much to be satisfied.

What gives satisfaction for a week may not do so for a year.

SAVAGE

Savages were little better than animals, and it is ludicrous to consider them laudable.

The savage still lurks in civilized mentality.

SAVING

Expenditure has very flexible limits, maximum or minimum. People can always save if they are prepared to do so, and the time to begin saving is from the beginning, when income is meagre.

Those who save money save themselves.

Savings make one feel more secure about one's future.

SAYING

If one says whatever one thinks, one will have a host of enemies.

One can say a lot in a few words or a little in a multitude of words.

SCANDAL

Scandal is scandalously enthralling to many a quiet citizen.

An affair bruited about becomes more unsavoury at the hands of fancy and malice.

SCAPEGOAT

The meddlesome busybody makes a good scapegoat.

It is easy to find a scapegoat.

One who does not wish to be a scapegoat should keep away from an affair.

SCENE

The best painting is a natural scene.

The multitudinous scenes perceived through the kaleidoscope of life make a delightful film.

The human scene traverses the gamut of emotions.

SCEPTICISM

Knowledge begins with scepticism.

The sceptic is not a cynical disbeliever but an earnest seeker after truth. His doubt is a weapon of inquiry.

SCIENCE

Nature has existed for countless ages; discoveries and inventions are already in it and are new only to humankind.

The pursuit of science without ethical aims is the cause of the parlous state of the world.

Science is common sense with uncommon results.

Science is not everything in life. Its importance is great but should not be exaggerated.

SCORN

The vulgar may scorn the sage on grounds of folly.

Magnanimous people scorn to scorn their inferiors.

The only rightful scorn is scorn of what is stupid or evil.

SCRAP

Social organization is bad when a section of the populace has to subsist on scraps.

To live on a scrap of hope is pathetic, but it is better than to have no hope at all.

A scrap of pleasure now and then sweetens the darkest life.

SCRUTINY

People are normally careless. If one doesn't like errors, one should scrutinize all work done on one's behalf.

SEARCH

A search is exciting and a successful outcome exhilarating. To combat ennui, embark on a search, whatever the object may be.

The search for truth is the greatest of adventures.

It is pleasant to search for something and find something else in addition.

SECRET

If you would keep a thing secret, tell nobody. If you can't keep a secret yourself, don't expect others to do it for you.

Revelation of a secret is delicious.

Secretiveness is the mark of the small mind.

The secrets of nature should be made manifest to all. It was the desire for secret knowledge that led to magic and esoteric cults and other forms of charlatanism.

SEEING

It's odd that one can see the whole of another thing but cannot see the whole of one's own person.

Different people see the same thing differently. The eye is merely an organ for conveying impressions to the mind, which registers them in its own way.

SEEMING

One is never exactly as one seems. The face does not reflect character like a mirror.

Humans are the only creatures who are not what they seem.

To seem bad and be good evokes initial condemnation and final approbation.

SEIZURE

Seizure of the right moment makes for success.

Those who never allow themselves to be seized by fits of passion are rational beings.

Seizure of a person by force for any purpose whatsoever is always bad.

SELF

Nobody is so interesting to a person as his own self.

It is impossible for people wholly not to care for themselves; such regard is not the reprehensible selfishness that takes little account of others.

The self is a mystery even to people themselves.

One's better self should not kowtow to one's worse self.

Each person does things that tend to destroy himself.

SELF-RELIANCE

Reliance on oneself entails the least disappointment.

In the last resort, everyone has to fall back on himself.

People should observe, read, and then think for themselves; they should personally do, if they can, what they consider important or urgent.

SENSUALITY

Men blame women for the troubles they bring upon themselves.

Sensuality has many insidious ways, including posing as art and calling itself modern.

It is absurd that, after thousands of years of civilization and learning to control their animal instincts, people should think that progress means concupiscence run riot.

SEPARATION

Distinct entities that came together tend to separate.

Lengthy separation from friends and relatives always leaves a pang of regret.

In the kaleidoscope of history, lands have joined together and have become separated almost invariably by force.

SERENITY

Serenity is not complete without joy.

Serenity is negative and would not at first sight appear to be anything worth cultivating. But it has its good in relieving the mind from the aches of passion.

Reasoning swims best in a calm sea.

SERIOUSNESS

Life is a serious comedy.

Seriousness should not be mistaken for profundity.

SERVICE

Service is a benefit to others. Average people would perform for gain a service they would not do otherwise. Not to recognize this basic trait of human nature and to attempt to create a society based on service as a duty is to beget the hypocrisy and the exploitation of the good by the bad and the simple by the cunning.

A service is a good, whatever the motive may be.

In a proper society, the person who is of greatest service to others should receive the greatest rewards.

SEX

Sex is a natural, unavoidable phenomenon, and there is no need to talk of it *ad nauseam*.

Animals don't have the sex problems and aberrations that modern people have.

SHADOW

The phenomena we see are but shadows of reality.

Most things that humankind struggles for are shadows.

The shadow of a great person is so long that it stretches over the centuries and may prevent successive generations from seeing the sun of truth.

When hope is lost, one sees only the dark shadow of a proposal.

SHAME

Shame hangs on judgment of value. A change in our appraisal of values alters the things of which we are ashamed.

We would be happier if we were ashamed of fewer things.

No one can disgrace a person who has not disgraced himself.

SHORE

The shore shapes the sea. Motive determines action.

SHOW

Much of the furniture of civilization is merely for show.

Everybody likes to show himself at his best in public. What is this but vanity?

SILENCE

Silence destroys good relationships; speak when needed.

If silence were golden, it is surprising that orators have attained fame.

A due balance of silence and speech makes the greatest sense.

One who has nothing to say has nothing worth saying.

SIMILARITY

All human beings are much alike, as they belong to the same species, but when making comparisons, we tend to maximize their differences and minimize their similarities.

Similarity is not stimulating.

SIMPLICITY

Simplicity, if it were nothing else, at least has the merit of comprehensibility.

Simplicity is one of the few qualities desirable in everything.

Whatever is methodical is simple.

Complexity grows out of simplicity.

Once an idea is clearly grasped, it becomes simple.

SINCERITY

People are sincere when it suits their purposes.

Sincerity is essential for a good society.

When a person makes a display of his sincerity, it is time to be on guard.

SKILL

A chicken should not presume to teach a duck how to swim.

SKY

The sky is the most beautiful of illusions.

Love of visible nature is best exemplified by contemplation of the phenomena of the sky.

SLAVERY

Slavery is the worst form of oppression ever devised by humanity.

Slavery is as much an evil to the master as the slave—misery to one and immorality to the other.

SLEEP

Sleep at any time it suits you and only the requisite minimum.

Sleep is a sorry end to a happy day.

People fear death but enjoy sleep, which is temporary death.

To slaves, sleep is their greatest solace.

The only person who fears sleep is the tyrant.

SLOGAN

The masses are not given to thought, and slogans provide them with the illusion of thought.

A slogan is a capsule of half-truth prescribed to stimulate action.

The best slogan is the one least followed.

SMELL

Most smells are unpleasant. A smell-less thing is the best for smell.

To have a dog's sense of smell is to lead a dog's life.

SMILE

A smile is not necessarily attractive. A smile of malice is ten times more sickening than a scowl.

The value of a smile depends on its intention.

A smile brought about by harmless happiness is the only likable smile. Any other kind is senseless or noxious.

SNEER

A sneer is the greatest disfigurement of the face.

A sneer is contempt made crooked by malice.

SOCIETY

Society is made for the individual, not the individual for society.

There will always be numerous classes in society corresponding to the variety of human characteristics.

SOLITUDE

The ability to enjoy solitude is a precious gift.

One can be more solitary in a city than in a village.

Preference for solitude to society gives more time for thought.

The free, dreamy breeze of solitude is incomparable.

SOLUTION

Every problem has a solution. We may not know it, but it's waiting to be found.

Solutions are easy once they are known.

Accidental solutions are just as acceptable as the deliberate, but reliance on them is precarious.

SORROW

Sorrow shows the world at its worst. The amount of sorrow experienced by humanity indicates the faultiness of life and the inadequate state of civilization.

Sympathy assuages sorrow but little.

It is as natural to be sad as to be happy. One can feel sad without any sufficient cause.

The knife of sorrow grows blunt with time.

Great art is inspired by sorrow.

SOUND

A speech without sense is just sound.

The sound of laughter can grate on the nerves.

Sound is the phenomenon *par excellence* for forcing itself on our attention against our will.

SPACE

Space is nothingness, yet it has properties. It is negative, yet it is a positive fact.

Space is the greatest expanse of homogeneity in the universe.

SPECTATOR

Contestants know only their own problems; spectators view all sides.

Spectators enjoy more than the participant in any activity, for they do not have to exert themselves.

SPEECH

The proper use of speech is to reveal thought; its improper use, to conceal it.

Speech should not be vacant of thought like a politician's.

An after-dinner speech is efficacious in countering the excitement of the feast—it is soporiferous.

One should speak only about what one understands.

A successful extempore speech belies its name.

A chance remark may reveal one's character better than one's usual behaviour.

A persuasive speaker wins applause and money.

The tireless listener is less common than the tireless talker, though he is more welcome.

SPEED

The inventions that most distinguish the modern age from preceding ages occur in the realm of speed.

Caeteris paribus, speedy work is preferable to slow work.

SPONGING

The sponger is always ready to share with his friends—what is theirs.

Sponging is a low art with as much dignity as a pig.

SPORT

There are two categories of sportsmen: those who play and those who watch others play.

The essence of sports is competition, and the last thing a sportsman wants is defeat with a smile.

Sport has become a profession, play a serious matter. If we cannot progress in one direction, we can always progress in the other.

STAR

To our commonsense observation, the stars are only twinkling points of light in the heavens; to romance, they are beautiful jewels or are counters for the telling of fortunes; yet they are each much more immense than the earth.

If a thousand stars were to pass out of existence, we would take it with equanimity; if the earth were to vanish, it would be the catastrophe of catastrophes.

STARVATION

The bayonet of starvation is the impelling force of humans and beasts.

The fact that there are people who starve and do not steal shows human nature at its best.

A starving person has no dignity.

STATE

A state can be greater than its inhabitants generally, but it cannot be better.

In a state, the strong are subject to the weak. Physically, the peasants and workmen are stronger than their rulers like monarchs, dictators, priests, scholars, and plutocrats.

STEAM

It is astonishing that the force of steam is more powerful than the strength of the biggest animal.

The steam from one boiler is the same as that from another. There is nothing to choose between them.

The steam of anger is more dangerous confined than released.

STEP

A step backward is a loss of two steps forward.

Progress by regular steps is the surest of all progress.

One wrong step is all that is needed for failure.

STORM

A storm is nature's burst of temper.

It is pleasant to listen to the sound of a storm but not to feel its force.

The storm of revolution tends to take its own course.

One cannot direct a storm or luck.

A storm in the mind shakes one more than a storm in the atmosphere.

STORY

A moral story is a bore; an immoral story is no better.

Many an entertaining story contains a revelation of nothing.

The first function of a story is to tell a story.

STRANGENESS

The strange is merely what you don't know.

What is strange is not accepted until it ceases to be strange.

One who can encounter strange things and ideas and is not repelled by them, but endeavours to understand and possibly accept them, has a rare, open, intellectual mind.

STREET

In life, there are quite a few one-way streets, notably that leading from birth to death.

A street is intended to be a way for going from one place, usually a building, to another. It has become more than that; it is an inferno of noise and death.

STRENGTH

Physical strength is extremely limited; humans are not even the strongest of animals.

Strength of character will see one through a host of troubles.

It is ludicrous for the strong to be under the control of the weak, though it is wrong for the strong to tyrannize over the weak.

STRUCTURE

Safety and economy are the twin foundations of a good structure.

Every scheme has a structure that should be well planned beforehand.

An ideological system should be like a structure in the interconnection of its ideas.

STRUGGLE

One may accept less than what one wants and then continue the struggle.

Life is one incessant struggle.

To struggle against nature is bad enough, but what is worse is the struggle between person and person.

The ferocious struggle for existence of living things is an unmitigated tragedy.

STUDY

Study for pleasure is more profitable than study for profit.

Each study has appropriate discipline and benefit.

Study moulds the intellect but not moral character.

Study will not make a genius, but it will make a genius learned.

The proper study of humankind is the universe.

STYLE

Style is an author's fingerprint.

A good style is that which reveals a distinctive personality.

Style will not turn nonsense into sense, but it will render it charming.

SUBJECTION

All people live in varying degrees of subjection.

To be conquered psychologically is a subjection worse than outward submission to force.

SUBSTITUTE

The original is never so highly valued as when one is compelled to accept a substitute.

It is more satisfactory in choosing a substitute to look to the requirements of the case than to consider resemblance to the original.

Substitutes are never appreciated, for if they are like the original, they are deemed an inferior imitator, and if they are different, they are said to be an inferior sort.

SUCCESS

The winner is the one who wins in the end.

The hill of success is difficult to scale.

Vulgar opinion equates success with intelligence and failure with stupidity—and so does scholarly judgment.

Success ill becomes the person who doesn't deserve it.

Success is the same whether the odds are for or against it, but the meritoriousness is different.

Success is proof of superiority and failure of inferiority—this criterion facilitates judgment!

An idea is successful when the populace at large believes it to be right without knowing why. A person is successful when many people think highly of him without understanding his achievements.

SUGGESTION

A suggestion must be carefully considered before adoption. A bucket must be tested for leakage before purchase.

Reject a suggestion carelessly and it may return to laugh at you.

Don't make suggestions lightly but take into account the consquences that may arise from them.

SUICIDE

Suicide is a disaster, not a crime.

Suicide spells the triumph of the present over the future.

No one commits suicide save under severe stress, and such a one is to be pitied, not condemned. It is commonplace for people to wish for death, but they seldom attempt to kill themselves.

SUITABILITY

Everything is suitable for something.

What is suitable for one thing is unsuitable for another.

Unsuitable suitability is the mistake of many a selector of candidates for jobs.

If you cut your coat according to your cloth, it may not fit; it is better to get a sufficient piece of cloth first.

SUPERSTITION

Superstition is momentous to the victim and ludicrous to the observer.

The power of superstition is not killed by reason.

Superstition is wrong belief imbibed in childhood.

Superstition is largely associated with religion because, like religion, it is irrational.

SUPPORT

The thread does not precede the needle; the stronger should support the weaker.

SURPRISE

If you walk along a muddy road, you shouldn't be surprised if you get soiled.

Surprise is the most effective of secret weapons.

SUSPICION

Suspicion poisons the well of social intercourse.

Suspicion lays snares where none exist.

Trust can be betrayed and suspicion can be wrong; no policy is foolproof.

SWITCH

Electric switches are so numerous that we would not know what to do with our fingers without them.

SYMBOL

The symbol is not the reality.

Great people are held in such esteem for their symbolic rather than their genuine importance.

SYMPATHY

Sympathy without action is mere luxury.

It is not easy to realize other people's condition, and sympathetic insight is necessary for a reasonable degree of understanding.

SYSTEM

A jumbled collection of ideas does not make a system; a tangled coil of strings does not make a net.

To be systematic is to keep error at bay.

The formulation of a system of thought is the greatest of intellectual tasks.

T

TACT

Tact is the art of avoiding injury to vanity.

The greater the tact, the less the embarrassment.

Tact is the easiest way of winning approbation.

Tact does not make people good but makes them good for society.

TAMENESS

Tame animals are eaten. Tameness invites disaster.

TASK

A task willingly executed is a treat.

However onerous the task, it is not so to one who likes it, and however facile, it is not so to one who dislikes it.

There is no lack of tasks to harass a person; it is wise to do what is needed and ignore the rest.

TASTE

Every kind of taste can be appreciated. Sweet food is not the most delicious.

Taste is more pleasurable than any other sense, for it can more easily avoid contact with unpleasant things.

The art of cookery is the art of taste.

To force one's taste on another is as futile as it is absurd.

TAXATION

No one loves taxes but everyone wants a government to execute works which benefit him. Steering between the Scylla of taxation and the Charybdis of service, no government is really popular.

It would be adding insult to injury to pretend that taxes are for the good of the taxpayer.

TEA

There have not been many discoveries that have become so cheap as to be available to the poorest person. Among them tea holds an outstanding place. It has promoted sobriety.

TEACHING

Teach people against their will and you teach them nothing.

One who has not learned well will not teach properly.

A good book makes a superb teacher.

One is one's best teacher.

TEAR

Tears are what make one realize that the world is not all that good.

The tears of life make its smiles seem hollow.

TEMPER

What makes one person mad makes another laugh.

Those with the worst tempers don't explode at their bosses. This goes to show that it is not too difficult to control one's temper.

Those who let their tempers run away with them injure themselves more than they injure others.

TEMPTATION

Temptation is of things desirable. Normally what one wants is something beneficial. Hence, it would seem that the rational course is to yield to temptation. But moral codes, public welfare, and the higher good make many desirable things undesirable.

Struggle with some temptations and avoid others; it depends on the nature of the evil and the consequence of failure.

Many people would like to fall victim to temptation if it would only come their way.

THEFT

One theft successful, more thereafter.

A thief does not ordinarily steal from another thief.

No one loves money more than a thief.

What is stolen may give a thrill of pleasure, but its possible untoward consequences will give a thrill much less pleasant.

THEORY

Theory and practice are like friends who are really enemies.

A theory may just be an admirable work of art with little relevance to truth.

A theory is good for various purposes, and if its truth is dubious, it may still be held, provided its real character is recognized.

THOUGHT

Thought is the mind at work.

The ordinary person's thoughts on any subject are not systematic but are mere ideas born of convention, prejudice, and ill-assorted knowledge absorbed from his environment.

Thought does not necessarily correspond with truth. A thing is not true or good merely because one believes it to be so. This sounds obvious, but most people behave as though reality must somehow be what they think.

Those who rarely think think when they think that they think profoundly.

THREAT

The more vociferous the threat, the less likely will it be executed.

An unuttered threat is a snake in the grass.

It is silly to make a threat that cannot be executed. Empty threats redound to the injury of the one making the threat.

THRIFT

To spend less is better than to earn more.

Thrift is the passport to wealth.

Thrift is the eschewal of what is not necessary.

Thrifty extravagance ill becomes anyone. To be thrifty generally and be extravagant over one or two things is worse than to spend reasonably on things as a whole.

THUNDER

Thunder frightens but works no injury. The danger lies in its twin brother, lightning.

TIME

How wonderful that we have learnt to measure intangible time by the tangible clock!

To us who have but a short time to live, every bit of time should be precious—and yet we squander it more wantonly than anything else.

Nothing is more inexorable than the even flow of time.

Time has no sound, save what humankind gives it by way of the ticking of a clock. Its silence makes its power overwhelming.

You cannot kill time; if you try, it will kill you.

TITLE

None loves titles more than those without any real worth in themselves.

A title is like a handle—useful in its trifling way but without any assurance of the soundness of an article.

TODAY

Today is the forerunner of tomorrow. Let us use today partly to prepare for tomorrow.

To live for today is right provided it is not wholly so.

We experience today and we'll have many more todays. It's absurd to try and live as if today is the last day of our life; if it were, there's still no cause for regret for having missed something, as we can never experience all we want.

TOIL

The incessant toil of the bee and the ant is silly.

Toil, unless it is a necessity imposed by conditions, is undesirable.

The good thing about machinery is not only that it is more efficient than human beings but also that it relieves them of unremitting drudgery.

TOLERANCE

Necessity makes the intolerable tolerable.

All human beings are essentially the same. What could happen to one person could happen to any person. If we realized this, we would learn to be tolerant.

TOOL

Tools are humankind's glory and disgrace. With them, we are master of our environment and all creatures, and murderer of our kind.

TOUCH

One cannot touch the sun but can feel its rays. One may not do great work but can be inspired by it.

If people could have a magic touch that granted them the kind of thing they wanted, the best would be the understanding touch.

TOURISM

A tourist is one who considers another people's ordinary ways as strange and their solemn ceremonies as amusing.

Tourism is mass interest in historical relics and scenic spots that the individual secretly thinks not worth seeing.

The pleasantest way to eliminate savings is to go on a tour.

TOWN

The town is the triumph of humanity over its environment.

If people want their activities to go unnoticed, they should live in a city; the more numerous the inhabitants, the more faceless they become.

The curse of a town is that it harbours wild people worse than those in the jungle.

TRADE

That those who sell should earn more than those who produce betrays the topsy-turvy character of society.

Trade is the brother of exchange.

Trade and trickery need not be inseparable.

TRADITION

A tradition came into being haphazardly and remained fixed.

Traditions are seldom right, for, even if they commenced as truths, they gathered accretions shortly thereafter and became erroneous.

A tradition is a belief of long standing still maintained for the reason that it is a tradition.

TRAFFIC

The tragedy of modern life is traffic.

Most motorists obey traffic rules because they consider them sensible and don't know how to violate them without finding themselves in trouble.

TRAGEDY

It is terrible to think that at this moment all round the world tragic occurrences and violent crimes are being enacted.

It is a tragedy when a wit finds his jokes received by an audience in severe solemnity.

Life is more of a tragedy than a comedy.

TRAVEL

Travel in the old days was an adventure; now it is a pastime.

The greatest benefit of travel is experience.

Ease of travel varies directly as speed of movement.

A traveller should not hesitate to ask questions.

TREASURE

Everyone hopes to find a treasure some day.

Greed varies directly as treasure.

Treasure invites theft.

TREATMENT

The world treats us according to our present circumstance, a little influenced by what we have done, not at all by what we may be able to do.

One person treats another according to their relative positions.

No matter what your treatment of a person may be, there are times when it is unsuitable.

One whose treatment of others is not as they deserve deserves similar treatment.

To progress, one has to treat oneself roughly.

TREE

Trees don't feel the urge to walk.

A tree is the personification of endurance.

A tree is life at peace.

A tall, slender tree swaying in the wind is an exemplar of enchanting gentleness and admirable toughness.

TRIFLE

Things that are trifles when considered singly are momentous when considered in the mass.

Preoccupation with trifles betokens the little mind.

A trifle may generate a serious effect.

Any pursuit is trifling to one who is not interested in it.

TROUBLE

We may evade trouble, but trouble will not evade us.

People talk about their troubles to win sympathy, but they would only get one more trouble if they could read their listeners' minds.

A fire that begins with one house spreads to others; trouble that begins with one person involves others.

TRUST

Trust is a precious commodity that few keep.

A trusted assistant is the one who commonly ousts a leader.

People do not become more trustworthy because they see that they are trusted or are told that they are trusted, but they become less trustworthy when the contrary is the case.

A stratagem relying on the victim's trust may be successful; however, it denotes not cleverness but baseness.

TRUTH

Truth is not the object of a court of law.

Truth is the most dangerous thing in the world.

Truth is what exists openly or secretly.

Truth knows no national boundaries.

There is no necessity that truth, any more than genius or murder, must ultimately be revealed.

Telling the truth is not always salutary as, for example, when one reveals to a desperado that one has seen him commit a murder.

TYPE

A person should strive to be an individual and not a type.

TYRANNY

Tyranny wears many forms and is not confined to the ruler of a state.

The tyrant close at hand is worse than one at a distance.

Tyrannical behaviour and stupid thought are often associates.

Freedom from tyranny spells undiluted joy.

U

UGLINESS

Ugly life has made beautiful art.

If our ideas of beauty are largely subjective, then what we think ugly may not be so.

One who is in an ugly mood will not listen to beautiful expression.

UNDERSTANDING

One stumbles who walks in the dark.

To understand oneself is difficult enough, what more to understand others!

To sympathize without understanding is better than to understand without sympathy.

Refusal to understand is more exasperating than stupidity.

It is absurd to subscribe to what one does not understand, yet this is the way of the common person in respect of religion and other subjects.

Primitive people made gods of the forces beyond their understanding.

UNIFORMITY

Uniformity sings a dull tune.

We are so perverse that, were all things uniformly good, we would long for defects to appear.

Uniformity in the matter of articles that require identical replacements, like electric light bulbs and motor vehicle accessories, is a necessity; but where it is not essential, it is undesirable.

UNIQUENESS

Nothing in the world is really unique. A thing is not unique merely because it is rare or admirable.

UNITY

Unity is an assemblage of harmonious parts.

A basic unity is all that is needed to make diversity meaningful.

When people sit around a dinner table talking in a lively manner, they are enjoying a feast and unity.

UNIVERSE

Humankind is a pathetic bit of the universe.

That a fragment of mind enclosed in a fragment of matter should be able to grasp the universe—that is the greatest wonder of all.

UNIVERSITY

The notion that a university course is the qualification without which one is incapable of practising a particular profession is a fallacy.

The best university is what one organizes oneself.

It's an expensive way of spending one's time to go to a university for that purpose.

It is a pity that there is no professorship of nonsense in a university. If there were, there would be no lack of qualified candidates from the existing staff for the post.

UNREST

Ours is the Age of Unrest; so was every other age.

Unrest, whether of individuals or nations, is motivated by the desire for wealth.

Unrest is greatest where frustration is dominant.

Intense unrest always precedes a revolution.

URGENCY

One should not go through life with the air of urgency pertaining to a telegram.

Urgency does not require fuss.

UTILITY

In practical life, utility comes before beauty. In the absolute scheme of values, the reverse is the case.

The test of an invention is its utility.

Utility and beauty should both be pursued in our material productions.

V

VACATION

A vacation can be more exhausting than work.

VACILLATION

One who is firm in naught save vacillation will reap firm failure.

One should not vacillate like a pendulum.

VALUE

We value our possessions for lack of better things.

Everything has two categories: the good comprising what we like and the bad what we dislike!

Nowadays people value modern ideas and ancient artefacts.

VANITY

So many things one does are to please others but are ultimately for the purpose of winning approbation and thereby pleasing one's vanity.

The monkey does not think it is ugly.

Vanity is a laughable foible that harms nobody.

One's vanities reveal one's system of values and the character of one's mind.

VARIETY

Variety is to monotony what joy is to misery.

Variety is sensible only when each variant has its distinctive good.

It is odd that nature, which is given to variety, should show the multitudinous stars in the sky as similar points of light.

VERBOSITY

To describe in detail the formation of a flower does not indicate its beauty. Verbosity only serves to miss the point.

VICE

Vice is vice, though it be called art.

Vice is a sword with a hilt of pleasure and a blade of pain.

Vice is pleasure gone wrong.

Vice is silly, for it is silly to destroy oneself.

VICTIM

Sympathy for the victim marks the noble nature.

Gullible victims need not be objects of ridicule; their trusting nature makes their deceivers objects of contempt.

VICTORY

If the objective is victory, then the principle sacred to heroes of victory or death does not sound enlightened, for where victory is palpably unattainable when one is alive, death will not achieve it either.

One's victory is another's defeat, and the joy of victory should be tempered with the sadness of sympathy.

Victory in war wears an ugly mien and a tattered coat.

A military victory leading to no considerable change in human affairs has about as much significance as a victory at the chess table or on the football field.

People are failures who, after a series of victories, end their careers with a catastrophic defeat.

VILLAGE

A village is a forlorn unit of habitation.

The village is a relic of barbarism.

VILLAIN

In real life, the villain is as likely to win as to lose. This does not speak well of the rightness of things or of society.

There are many more crooks operating within the law than outside it.

Everyone has some use, even a villain, without whom there would be no hero.

VIOLENCE

Violence breeds greater violence.

Violence is a relic of savagedom.

One who lives by violence dies by it.

The violence of the most violent acts of nature is less horrible than the violence of human beings.

VIRTUE

Virtue is as much a resident of the mind as of action.

Virtue is practised for all sorts of reasons, from health to business. The most sublime motive is ethical good.

In a degenerate age, virtue is doubly precious.

Virtue is what people wish others to possess in greater measure than they themselves do.

VISIT

A visit is only as pleasant as the host makes it.

A visit to a strange place is exciting, to a familiar place soothing.

VOLCANO

A volcano is nature's way of letting off steam.

VULGARITY

Vulgarity is the ugliest of faults.

W

WAGER

Wagering is the sister of gambling.

A wager won is as bad as a wager lost.

WAITING

Those who sit and wait will forever be waiting for whatever they are waiting for.

Waiting is never an easy load.

Whatever the outcome of waiting may be, time is lost.

A couple of vexations are constantly around: one is waiting for something that turns up and the other for what doesn't.

The unconscionable way that law courts have of making people wait is in itself an outrage.

WAKING

To wake up is easy when there is someone to drag you out of bed.

To lie awake in bed cogitating for some time before getting up is a pleasant and profitable way of spending time.

WALKING

Walking is the only universal exercise, and it's the best.

A walk alone is better than a walk in company, if only because one is free to do as one likes.

WAR

War is a relic of barbarism and has no redeeming feature; its waste, ugliness, stupidity, and cruelty are monstrous.

The ordinary person is not less prone to war than kings.

If war were not so common, we would regard warriors as psychopathological cases.

The inglorious glory of war has captured the imagination for far too long.

To regard war as an interesting game of chess or a captivating subject for an epic or a necessity for the flowering of certain virtues shows to what depths the mind can sink.

WARNING

A warning is the herald of hostilities and should never be disregarded.

A warning is half as bad as the actual event.

A warning that cannot be implemented is worse than no warning.

WASTE

Those who are running their wasteful way to bankruptcy will have regret for their companion.

Waste goes hand in hand with public ownership.

Waste is the concomitant of inefficiency.

WATER

The sound of lapping waves on the shore and the sound of falling rain constitute the music of water.

Nature shows its fine sense of discrimination when it makes the ready availability of food, water, and air follow their comparative necessity to life.

Even the drinking of water is fraught with peril.

WAVE

The wave endows the sea with its entrancing beauty. One feature can serve to make or mar a phenomenon.

The wave in the atmosphere bears no resemblance to the sound it engenders. Dissimilarity need be no bar to association.

WEAKNESS

A weak will is more deleterious than a weak body.

The greatest joy of the bully is the suppliant weakling who never thinks of retaliation.

WEALTH

Wealth is a matter of comparison. If everyone had little, none would be poor; if all had much, none would be rich.

If one is rich, one is hated; if poor, despised.

Two things are detrimental to the welfare, whether of a nation or an individual: one is to have too little and the other to have too much.

One does not acquire great wealth without enterprise and chance.

Wealth is not necessary for a satisfactory life.

WELCOME

Welcome accorded determines happiness generated.

The most humiliating tragedy is when a defeated populace lines up to welcome a conquering army.

Many a welcome is more distressing than many a farewell, for they spell the beginning and end of an unwelcome relationship respectively.

WELFARE

In a welfare state, the rich make money for the benefit of the poor.

Welfare that does not denote personal happiness is delusive.

WHISPER

A whisper is not a natural mode of talking and its objective is to prevent others from hearing what one has to say. It only serves to excite suspicion.

Whispering magnifies a secret or makes a secret out of what isn't one.

The behaviour of a whisperer looks comical.

The whispering sounds of nature are expressions of its gentleness and contain no hint of injurious secrecy.

A whisper is as unattractive as a bluster.

WILL

Will is the sovereign of the mind.

To let the will sleep, one might as well sleep for good.

Whether the will is really free or not, one behaves as though it is.

WIND

The wind is a symbol of invisible strength.

The wind is more captivating as a feeling than as a sound.

The wind sends leaves spinning away; reason makes fancies float into nothingness.

WISDOM

Wisdom is knowledge of the universe.

Wisdom is what few people care to possess.

Wisdom is the only commodity of which one cannot have enough.

It is better to be wise and unhappy than stupid and happy.

One million fools don't think as correctly as one sage.

WISH

When one wish is fulfilled, make another; people will thus never be contented, but they will be alive.

Work is the key to the attainment of a wish.

Wishes should not run rampant.

WIT

Wit that leaves a sting is best left unsaid.

Few wits are witty.

WITNESS

One does not call a witness to tell the truth against oneself.

Ten witnesses tell ten different stories.

The most loquacious witness is the least reliable.

WOMAN

Women are human beings and are neither better nor worse than men.

The best man can find a woman to love him; so can the worst.

WONDER

Wonder does not endure long but soon terminates in acceptance or rejection.

Wonder comes from ignorance and unfamiliarity.

WORD

An opportune word can save an awkward situation.

Words are ideas in frames.

Words must be carefully watched, lest they act like poisoned darts.

WORK

If there were no work, the world would be completely different.

When people work for others, they are working for themselves.

People work to live; some live to work at intellectual tasks they consider important.

All work issues in physical form. All physical work entails at least some physical strength, even wielding a pen.

The modern ideal is to work as little as possible for as much as possible.

Many a busy person makes one think of the tremendous load.

Work as a matter of course is more productive than work by fits and starts.

Honey is sweet, but it is the accumulation of untiring bees. A good product is the result of hard work.

WORLD

If ours were the only inhabited world and matter were made for life, nature's prodigality would be inefficiency at its worst.

The world has become small; wherever we go, we are likely to encounter past acquaintances.

If we could choose, how many would prefer to live in a sorry world like ours?

WORRY

Be wary of futile worry.

WOUND

A physical wound leaves a scar that is only a blemish, while a mental wound leaves a scar that continues to hurt.

Life is ever ready to wound us with its knife.

WRITING

Writing is deliberate speech.

The written word is dangerous. It serves as a memorandum for you and as ammunition for your opponent.

WRONG

Imitation of what is wrong is idiotic and common.

Those who are always in the wrong must have something wrong with them.

To be right when all the world is wrong is an achievement; to be wrong when all the world is right is an achievement too.

Wrong has triumphed more than right.

Begin wrong and end right; this is better than the other way about.

X

XENOPHOBIA

Xenophobia should retreat before humanity and progress.

Xenophobia would vanish, were the world a single state.

Xenophobia is the product of prejudice. It springs from the inability to understand the unfamiliar and the absurd notion that all one's own ways are the best in the world. In olden times, when, owing to difficulties of travel, the nations were steeped in mutual ignorance, xenophobia was explicable; nowadays, it is unpardonable.

X-RAYS

X-rays emphasize the mystery of nature.

Y

YEAR

A year is so short, yet it contains 365 days—quite a number.

We may be worse next year, but we may also be better—why worry?

YEARNING

Yearning does not mean getting.

Yearning is the poor relative of possession.

Yearning is a futile pastime unless it acts as a spur to action.

YIELDING

One who never yields is unconquerable.

To yield to circumstance is not shameful, but to continue to struggle is heroic.

YOUTH

Youth is the beginning of life, not its all in all.

The absurd overrating of the importance of youth engenders the ludicrous result of self-torture, worrying about one's age and getting more and more afraid and ashamed of it as the years pass. Nothing shows more one's capacity for gratuitously inflicting suffering on oneself.

Youth is the period of experiment on a diversity of activities.

Z

ZEAL

Zeal is the uncle of success. It promotes it, but it is not the only cause, for ability and opportunity are important factors too.

Cultivate sustained zeal rather than spasmodic zeal.

Zeal must be directed by thought.

Beware that zeal does not make use of the wrong means or work for the wrong end.

The stupid can be just as zealous as the intelligent.

ZIGZAG

The zigzag line is more picturesque and perplexing than the straight.

ZOO

It would be laughable if evolution ends with all animals in the zoo.

Life is a spectacle, the greatest evidence of this being the assembling of animals in a zoo.

However kindly treated animals in a zoo may be, they would prefer freedom in their natural habitats.

About the Author

Born around the time of the foundation of the Republic of China, in the former English colony of British Malaya, Tan Kheng Yeang was educated in an English school. His father was from China but had immigrated to Malaya and had become a successful businessman, involved in various activities, including the rubber industry. From his early days, the author was interested in literature and philosophy, and as his interest evolved to science, he decided to study civil engineering at the University of Hong Kong, as he felt he needed a practical career.

After the Japanese occupied Hong Kong, he went into free China, where he found work in an office constructing roads and later an airfield in Guangxi Province. After the war ended in 1945, he returned to Malaya, became an engineer in the city council of Georgetown, Penang. After his retirement, he worked as an engineering consultant. He is the author of twelve books that reflect the broad range of his interests and talent.